WANTER DYNAMICS &
THE LOVE WE ARE

WANTER DYNAMICS & THE LOVE WE ARE

MITCH ROSACKER

ARIA DEVI

SELF DISCOVERY STUDIO

To all the people I have had the great honor of sitting with and sharing the journey with over the years.
It has been a great joy to watch you flower into your loveliness.
Shine On You Lovely Diamond!

PREFACE

From the moment I began exploring the nature of reality with Mitch Rosacker five years ago, I knew he would eventually write a book. In those early years of exploration, I never imagined I'd be supporting him in bringing his life-changing work into the world in this way.

Like many, I found my way to Mitch during a time of longing. I was in my twenties—staying in a relationship that didn't serve me, building a business I was no longer passionate about, and feeling completely disconnected from the Divine. There was a deep heartache I wasn't sure would ever go away.

I began exploring with Mitch in three-hour sessions—the same format he has practiced for over 25 years with people from all walks of life. Between those weekly sessions, I immersed myself in the daily practices and chanting Mitch suggested, many of which you'll find in this book.

Slowly, something began to shift. The identities I once clung to—like life rafts in a storm—began to unravel. The part of me that believed she had to be beautiful to be enough. The one who found her worth in how hard she worked, or how much money she made. The one who always had it together.

While these identities had served a purpose at one point in my life, I began to realize they weren't who I truly was.

We all pick up identities we cling to along the path. They become what we defend, the hills we die on. Whatever your life raft looks like, what once protected you can eventually become a cage. The more I leaned into my explorations with Mitch and the practices he offered, the less attached I felt to those identities and rafts.

I committed to being in the practices daily: Name That Thought Practice. The Living Practice (so much Living Practice). The Loving Blessing Practice. I began chanting in Sanskrit and studying texts like the *Pratyabhijñā Hṛdayam*. Over time, what was no longer mine to hold fell away. I left the relationship. I walked away from the business. And most importantly, I began experiencing life through a different lens—one of peace, calm, and love.

As I stabilized more and more in what Mitch calls True Nature, he and I would occasionally play with the idea of future books he might write. After one particularly transformative session, I felt a pull to write. Mitch invited me to connect with a beautiful orange and yellow image he had painted years ago. He said, "Just see what words come." What I wrote that day was the spark that unlocked the door back to writing.

I began writing daily. Less than a year later, I had written several manuscripts and published my first book. At some point, I realized that perhaps I was meant to support Mitch in writing his. With him so devoted to sitting with fellow explorers, taking a year off to draft a book would have pulled him from his dharma. But over the years, Mitch had recorded thousands of stories, chants, and ancient teachings that had already supported countless people. Those recordings became a treasure trove. The book was already there—it just needed transcribing. I offered to do it so those without the chance to sit with him one-on-one could still receive the wisdom that has changed so many lives.

While transcribing, there were moments when my entire body would heat up. The Shakti, in his words, was overwhelming. My spine would tingle, energy would shoot through my crown chakra. I had past-life memories. At times, I experienced Mitch's memories as if they were my own. There were days I had to stop writing altogether and rest from the intensity. These transmissions didn't just change my outer life—they transformed my inner world. And I believe they have the power to do the same for you.

Mitch and I carefully curated the recordings for this first book to support those navigating the dynamic play between The Wanter and True Nature—one of the primary dynamics we all experience that can create either suffering or liberation. There were hundreds of iterations of the title, contents, and structure. Every ounce of energy channeled into this book was intentional and offered in loving service. When it came time to discuss the cover of *Wanter Dynamics & The Love We Are*, we returned to the same vibrant orange painting Mitch had shared with me—the very image that sparked my return to writing, so clearly representing this play between The Wanter and True Nature.

You can read this book cover to cover, listen to the accompanying audio experience, or simply open it at random each day and receive the wisdom. However you approach it, this offering will meet you where you are. What we encourage most is this: learn these simple practices. Use them in your daily life. As Mitch's teacher from the Ashram used to say, "Just keep showing up for the practices—they will bear fruit." Those who stay with the practices often experience radical change in their lives and relationships. They begin to live with less suffering, more peace, more joy, more contentment—and love. So much love. That is the lovely possibility.

This isn't the only path to discovering your True Nature—that eternal, peaceful, compassionate, loving part of yourself—but it is one I live and love deeply, and one that hundreds of others have embraced. To me, these transmissions hold the power to shift consciousness in a deeply beneficial way. They can raise the frequency of the planet and help co-create a new kind of world:

A world that is unified.

A world that is at peace.

A world that is One.

A world that is pure love frequency.

I honor you for finding your way here. I hope this offering serves you as deeply as it has served me, and so many others Mitch has explored with.

Fellow traveler,
    Aria Devi

AUTHOR'S NOTE

THIS BOOK IS COMPOSED OF TRANSCRIBED TEACHINGS ORIGINALLY recorded and shared by Mitch Rosacker with his students. Each chapter is drawn from a live audio recording and has been intentionally preserved in a near word-for-word format. While lightly edited for clarity, the integrity of his spoken word remains intact. Because each teaching was delivered as a complete offering, you may notice repeated stories or overlapping concepts—each stands on its own.

For those who wish to experience the original recordings, they are available on all major streaming platforms, YouTube, and at TheLoveWeAre.com

All supporting works connected to this book are carefully managed and maintained by those who explore with Mitch. A glossary has been included to provide clarity on Sanskrit terms and to explain the purpose of the practices referenced throughout the text.

I ALWAYS KNEW THAT I WAS LOVED

ALL I KNOW FOR SURE IS THAT I LOVE YOU WITH ALL MY HEART.

That is how it was for me growing up with my mom: I always knew that I was loved.

My earliest memory was when I was three years old. We were at the back of the house - a *very* small, *very* modest house. We were very poor. I was watching her digging in the dirt with a shovel. As she cut into the earth, she revealed a whole other world underneath: rocks, roots, worms, bugs, and dirt. I had a yellow plastic shovel, and I was trying to help her as best I could. She was digging out an area to plant vegetable seeds for us, so hopefully we would have something to eat. After preparing the area, she sat down, took off her shoes and socks, rolled up her pant legs just below her knees, and pressed her bare feet into the soil.

She sat on the ground with her feet flush with the earth. I was so inspired by how playfully she did this that I followed her example. I took off my little three-year-old shoes and socks, rolled up my pant legs, and placed my feet in the dirt. I sat down next to her. She was to my left and I was to her right.

She leaned back on her elbows, looked up at the sky and

was in bliss. I did the same. When I closed my eyes, I could feel her communicating with me without using her voice. It was my first experience of what we might call telepathy. I didn't know the word then. I doubt my mom did either. But she was inviting me into something. I could feel her saying: *Feel this. Be here. There is power in the earth.*

I began to feel a pulsation in the tips of my toes. It felt like a loving, nurturing mother's energy. I could feel it pulsing through my feet, up my ankles, flowing up my legs. It was like I was a flower. In that moment, I realized that all growing things are expressions of this loving, nurturing, pulsating energy that is the Earth.

This was what it was like to be with her, my mom. We would play. She would invite me into being fully available to life and all of its depth.

When I was four or five, we were in a grove of aspen trees. She was looking up at the wind and holding on to the trunk of a tree. She noticed how the leaves were moved by the wind. I put my hands on the tree. I was standing nearby, looking up at the leaves. I began to notice how the wind was moving them. Then I noticed that the branches were moving, the limbs were moving, and even the trunk of the tree I was holding was slowly swaying as the wind flowed up into the leaves.

After a long silence, she looked at me with such wonder and said, "Mitch, have you noticed that you can't actually see the wind? You become aware of its presence by the effect it has on other things."

One day, we were sitting by a river. I was about five years old at the time. We were sitting on a grassy bank, right next to the water, and I started to notice how nuanced the sounds of a river actually are when you really make yourself fully available. The smells. The sounds. The way the light shimmered on the surface. The energetic feeling of really being with the river. The power. The majesty.

She said to me, "I wonder how fast the water is actually moving."

She looked around and found a leaf, then repositioned her body to lean out over the water. She held on to the grass with her left hand, and with her right hand, she held the leaf just above the surface of the river and waited. She held it there. Just when I felt she was about to let go, she did.

The leaf fell into the river and flowed very quickly in front of us, from left to right.

She sat back and said, "Wow. It's moving a lot faster than I thought it would." Then she said, "The life of that leaf is now part of the river. Whatever the flow of the river is, the leaf is now merged with that energy."

Then you could see it—she had an insight. Her eyes widened, and she said, "Like us. We are like the leaf. We choose to fall into this river of life, and we become part of the energy of this life river."

As we continued our journey together, there was no father in my life. He left when I was a baby. My mom was pregnant with my younger sister at that time, and I tried to help with the need we had for money. I was born in 1958. My mom was nineteen when she had me. She didn't have a college education, and there weren't many opportunities in our small farming town in southern Colorado.

The first way I found to help was to get a bicycle paper route, delivering newspapers early in the morning. I saved enough money to buy a lawn mower and started mowing neighborhood lawns to make a little extra money. This was back when a gallon of gas cost twenty-five cents. I'd go to the gas station with my little red gas can, fill it up, and pay with a single quarter.

As we went through life together, I began to understand that the only way I could go to college was with a scholarship. Luckily, I was really good at sports. I got a baseball scholarship in my senior year of high school, and that's how I got into college.

My freshman year of college was 1976. On the first day of baseball practice, the guy I was warming up with and I had a wonderful conversation as we tossed the ball back and forth, getting ready for practice. After practice, he came up to me and said, "Mitch, you seem really open-minded. There's something I learned from my parents that I do every day. I don't usually share it because some people make fun of it or say it's weird, but I'd really like to share it with you. Would you like to know what it is?"

"Absolutely," I said. "What is it that you want to share?"

"Have you ever heard of meditation?" he asked.

"No," I said. "What is meditation?"

"Come to my room after practice and I'll teach you."

Yes! I said yes.

He lived right down the hall from me. We were all in the same dorm, all athletes. I knocked on his door. He secreted me into the room quickly. We were going to secretly meditate. I can only imagine what else was going on in the other rooms that day.

He went on to tell me that his parents had traveled through India and learned meditation from a guru there.

"What is a guru? And tell me all about India and meditation."

Which he did.

It turned out that his parents had learned a particular style of meditation during their travels, and they had shared it with him. Now he was sharing it with me. It was so wonderful. It was the beginning of my journey with what we call meditation— and I realized that all my life my mom had been teaching me this, even though we didn't call it meditation.

Another very significant event occurred during my freshman year in 1976. One day, one of the guys on the baseball team was late for practice. I went to check on him, and when I asked him why he was late, he said, "I soloed."

I looked at him, confused. "What does that mean? What do you mean, you soloed?"

"When you learn to fly airplanes, after many hours of instruction with your flight instructor, they let you fly the plane all by yourself," he explained. "It's called your solo flight."

I remember asking him, "How do you have time to play baseball, go to class, do your homework, *and* learn to fly airplanes?"

"Mitch, it's my major."

"We have a major here at our college where you learn to fly airplanes?" I asked.

He nodded. "Oh yeah, it's called Aeronautical Science."

Wow. So I changed my major.

I had my first experience in an airplane. We were so poor growing up that I had never flown anywhere.

I loved it right away—the perspective of being above the earth, seeing everything for miles, and the freedom of riding the wind. This invisible force that no one can see, and yet it has the power to lift and move something as massive as an airplane. I would ride the updrafts as the air flowed up cliff faces or along mountain ranges.

I loved it so much that I went all in. I earned my private pilot's license, my commercial pilot's license, and my instrument rating. You have to be able to fly in bad weather if you want to be a professional pilot, and I knew that was what I wanted to be. I ended up becoming a flight instructor.

One day, one of my own instructors pulled me aside and said, "Mitch, if you really want to give yourself the best chance of becoming a professional pilot, you should transfer to another college. It's in Daytona Beach, Florida. It's called Embry-Riddle Aeronautical University."

I got the forms in the mail, filled them out, and he wrote me a wonderful letter of recommendation. I mailed everything back, and weeks later, I got a letter in the mail. I had been accepted.

The next thing I knew, I was at Embry-Riddle Aeronautical University on this very unusual and unexpected journey. It didn't take me long to realize that the school offered all kinds of engineering classes—I was in heaven. I enjoyed them so much because I had always been curious.

All my life, I had been asking: *What is the True Nature of all this? How does an airplane really fly? How do the radios we use to communicate and navigate really work?*

I started taking avionics courses. I wanted to understand how we navigate using radio waves, how communication systems are built, how energy moves invisibly through the atmosphere, and somehow guides our path.

When you fly from one airport to another, you dial the frequency of the airport you're going to. Each airport has a building that emits energy into the atmosphere at a specific frequency—its own unique signal. Your aircraft's antenna picks up that signal and relays it to an instrument panel. That panel has a needle. As long as the needle stays centered, you're right on course. If it veers left or right, you're off course. So you adjust your course to get it back in the center. It's like flying on an invisible highway of radio waves, all the way to your destination.

I was captivated by it all. I wanted to learn more and more.

One day, after an avionics class, my professor came up to me and said, "Mitch, you've taken way more engineering classes than you need for your aeronautical science degree. Have you ever considered switching to avionics engineering?"

I asked him, "What would my career options be if I did that —if I switched to avionics?"

He said, "There are a lot of Embry-Riddle graduates working at the Kennedy Space Center on the Space Shuttle program. There's a good chance you could work on the Space Shuttle after you graduate."

I could hardly believe it. So I changed my major to avionics. And I ended up working at Kennedy Space Center on the Space Shuttle program. I got to be a part of incredible projects: the Hubble Space Telescope, the Magellan probe, the Galileo probe, satellites, and even some top-secret missions that I can't talk about—even today. It was surreal.

Here I was, a kid from a small farming town in southern Colorado, working on some of the most advanced aerospace projects in the world. It was the ultimate dream job—every day was filled with wonder. And through it all, I was still meditating.

One day, we were at Launchpad 39A at the Kennedy Space Center, running tests in a secure room directly under the space shuttle. During the tests, another department ran into a problem, and everything was put on hold. We were told it would be three or four hours before they could fix the problem.

Normally, in situations like this, we'd all pack up, leave the safe room, head back to the main buildings, and wait for a call to come back. But on this day—another life-changing day—I made a different decision.

As everyone was getting ready to leave, one of my fellow engineers turned to me and asked, "What are you doing? It's going to be three or four hours."

I said, "I'm going to stay."

He looked surprised. "Really?"

"Yes," I said.

"Okay," he said, and they left.

Now it was just me—alone in that top secret room underneath the Space Shuttle at Launchpad 39A. I settled into meditation. As I closed my eyes, I became aware that right above me was the space shuttle itself. For decades, we had been launching matter into space from this very spot. And I wondered: *Could I open up to this energy? Could I move vertically —consciously—into space?*

The moment I asked the question, it happened. I was out of my body. It was the first time I had ever experienced being out of the body. I could see myself sitting in the chair under the shuttle with my eyes closed.

Suddenly, I was above the space shuttle, seeing the launch pad from above. Then over Florida. Then over the Earth. I continued to expand outward—through the solar system, among the planets—no longer feeling any sense of separation. I was the solar system. I was the galaxy. I was the universe. Then I became aware of something even more vast: infinite universes. And I was one with it all. No distance, no separation —just Oneness. A single, elegant, eternal wholeness expressing itself in endless forms.

In that moment, I knew this was the Truth. All of us, everyone and everything, are unique expressions of the same divine totality. That experience . . . *that* was the real reason I was here in this human life. To remember. To know. And to share it somehow.

I sat there wondering, how could I ever explain this to anyone else? How could I convey this truth to the world? This realization—this desire to share what I now knew to be real— became the beginning of a whole new path.

Eventually, I left that ideal life as an engineer at the Kennedy Space Center. After a series of mystical events that would make this story very long, I found my way to Boulder, Colorado's Naropa Institute, founded by Chögyam Trungpa Rinpoche, who was a teacher from Tibet. It began as an institute of higher learning offering graduate degrees in the helping professions, leading to master's degrees in therapy. The college also integrated Tibetan Buddhist teachings into their degrees.

That summer, I was accepted at Naropa in Boulder, Colorado. I was told about a weekend celebration and, as an incoming student, I could attend if I was interested. I eagerly replied, "Yes, I'm interested. Where do I go and when does it start?"

They told me where the Friday night event would be. These were the days when you had to pull out a map to find your way —there was no internet or smartphones. I ended up being half an hour early for the event that Friday night in the summer of 1998. I walked into the meeting hall and saw a group of people with brown skin, dressed in vibrant clothing, setting up unusual-looking musical instruments on stage. They felt strangely familiar to me. I had the urge to join them, and as I walked up the steps toward the stage to sit with my new friends, I suddenly realized, *What are you doing? You need to sit in the audience.* So, I did. I took a seat right in front of them and watched as they arranged their fascinating instruments. As more and more people arrived, the event began at 7:00 p.m. They told us we would be chanting in Sanskrit: *Om Namah Shivaya.*

It was so familiar to me—how could I know this? And yet I knew it. We started, and I began to sob. It was like going home, immersed in the melody, the vibration of the beautiful chant, *Om Namah Shivaya. Om Namah Shivaya.* The sound of the drum, this small box that the person was sitting at, this organ-like instrument that I later learned was called a harmonium, the chimes, and the stringed instrument that I later learned was called a tambura. All so familiar.

As the energy in the gathering hall, where we all chanted together, grew and grew, I wondered: *Could I ride this energy, like what had happened at Launchpad 39A at the Kennedy Space Center?*

The next thing I knew, I was expanding—out, out, out—and I was out of my body again, seeing my body from above, all of us gathered together chanting, *Om Namah Shivaya*. Then I became aware of the building, Colorado, the Earth, the solar system, the galaxy, the universe, and the universes. In that moment, I realized this is a way that has been directly experienced for thousands of years: We are all one.

I cried, I laughed, and we chanted. We chanted for 45 minutes and then sat in meditation for another 45 minutes. It was so familiar: expanding into cosmic Oneness. After an hour and a half, I heard them ringing some chimes. It was so gentle, a way to gradually return to the body.

Someone came and sat right next to me, and I could feel her nurturing, loving energy. I could also feel an inner realm communication from her, as I had experienced with my mother. Telling me to take my time and not to feel rushed in opening my eyes.

About fifteen minutes later, I finally opened my eyes, and the woman next to me looked at me with such kindness and gentleness and asked, "Are you okay?"

"Yes, thank you so much for checking on me."

"Well, of course," she said. Then she asked, "Are you aware that you emanate light?"

I laughed, "What?"

"Are you aware that you emanate light?" she asked again.

"No. I wasn't aware of that."

"Well, you do." Then she said very playfully, "Who are you?"

I replied, "Mitch."

She laughed, "That's not the name I know you by."

I knew immediately that we had known each other forever —an old friend, a reunion.

We hugged, and cried, and she looked at me and said, "It is time for you to have a teacher."

I could feel the "yes" within me, knowing that whatever it took to find my way to this teacher, it was a yes.

She told me that she had been studying with a female guru from India for ten years. *Yes, yes.* It was so clear to me—yes, a female guru. All my life I had learned from my mom, my grandma Inga from Norway, my Aunt Shirley, Aunt Didi, Aunt Leslie, Aunt Ruth, and Aunt Karen. It was the *women* in my life who had been there for me and helped me learn how to navigate this place, and now I was invited to learn from a female guru from India.

Within two weeks, I was at the ashram.

I was there with my son Alan. We were supposed to stay for a week, but we ended up staying longer. We stayed for about a month that first summer. It just felt so familiar to me—the chanting, the meditation, the ancient texts, the food, the culture—it was amazing.

When we returned that fall, I started my first semester at Naropa, in a three-year master's program in transpersonal counseling psychology. There, we learned psychology, Buddhist teachings, and everything you need to become a therapist. Each fall and spring, I would do coursework for my master's degree and, in the Summer, my son Alan and I would go to the ashram.

When I finished my master's degree three years later, I was chanting an ancient Sanskrit text called the *Pratyabhijñā Hrdayam*, and during that experience, it was revealed to me that I couldn't work within the structure of the world of therapy, which came as a surprise. I had just completed a three-year master's degree to become a therapist, and it was very clear during that chanting that I was to continue to go to the ashram and not do therapy. It was crystal clear.

I followed that guidance even though it didn't make logical sense. After seven summers of going to the ashram, one day, through a very mystical event that would make this story *even* longer, my teacher moved me along to a different teacher. I didn't get to go to the ashram anymore.

I was with this teacher for a while, and then she wanted me to meet *her* teacher. Both of these teachers introduced me to other teachers. This went on for another four years, with eleven more teachers from many different lineages around the world.

One day, after those eleven years, I realized that my journey in searching for the Truth had come to an end. I was abiding in that realization, and knew that my time with the teachers was complete. So I began to go to my art studio every day to paint. Art has always been a spiritual practice for me, all my life. I would go into the studio, invite Grace, and let art be a way of connecting to the infinite source of all creation. Paintings would emerge. I imagined that I would go out and be an artist, sharing this sacred art that was coming through me with the world.

One day, while I was in the midst of a very powerful art experience with a painting I call *Heart of Being*, my phone rang. I wiped my hands, walked over to the wall where the phone was, and answered it. It was someone who knew me from one of the spiritual lineage groups I had been a part of.

She said, "Mitch, I'm so glad you were able to answer my call. I was just meditating, and I had a vision that I was sitting with you. You were teaching me practices that you learned at the ashram, telling me stories of your journey, sharing your experiences, and we were chanting together. Would this be possible?"

Yes, I could feel the "yes" of that. I told her, "Yes, come over."

We arranged the day and time, and before she arrived, I invited Grace, as I had learned to do in the ashram. We would do what's called an invocation, where you invite Grace. That day, I asked, "Please allow me to be the purest instrument of Grace that I can be. Please allow this to be beneficial for her. Please allow my attention to rest in the absolute love that I am and allow her to be released from the limitations of her mind. Allow her to directly experience her True Nature, so that she can release this love that she is, and allow her True Nature to shine into the world, in whatever way is most beneficial for her and others."

She arrived, I served her tea, and we explored the nature of reality. I ended up sharing a few practices with her that I learned at the ashram. We talked, and laughed, and cried. After about four hours, she said to me, "Oh my gosh, can I come back in a few days?"

"Absolutely," I said.

"Can I mention this to one of my friends?" She asked.

"Sure," I said. So her friend came in and we explored together.

Then her friend asked if she could tell her friend.

That friend came in and asked, "Can I tell my friend?"

Over the years, people have mentioned me to their friends, and I have been able to explore the nature of reality with so many amazing seekers of truth. All these years I've had the great honor of exploring how life itself is the very playground where we can discover who we really are, and let that be lived. There are natural ways that I've learned on my journey, and I share them with everyone. I'm honored and filled with joy and awe to share this with all of you.

WANTER DYNAMICS & THE LOVE
WE ARE

WELCOME. WELCOME TO PLANET EARTH. IT'S BUCK WILD HERE.

If we let ourselves be playful for a moment—which is always fun to do—we can consider that these human lives we are living are an exploration of the play of separation: the play of 'there's me and other,' 'there's self and other,' the play of duality. When, in the deepest truth, we never actually leave the wholeness that we are—the love that has no conditions, the absolute kindness and wisdom and clarity. We always will be this.

And yet, we get captured in this aspect of consciousness that I call: The Wanter.

Here we are, in this University of Consciousness. If we let ourselves be playful, we can say we're taking an advanced class that we could call Wanter Dynamics. We're exploring the dynamic characteristics of The Wanter—this aspect of consciousness that is our ally. When we're experiencing our human life, our Wanter is always trying to make things ideal for us, to optimize the moment, to ensure our survival. That is its very nature. It's always self-oriented.

This is why, when we're captured in our Wanter, we can be

very selfish, uncaring about others, always trying to make things better for ourselves through manipulative or controlling behaviors.

There is so much suffering that we experience when we're captured in our Wanter. When we don't get our way, when it doesn't go how our Wanter wants it to go, we have a disturbance. It might be annoyance, frustration, anger, or even rage. It can amplify into resentment, regret, or self-loathing.

From here, we often try to get some sort of external stimulus to bring a feeling of ease: we want someone to comfort us, to give us attention, to confirm us, to love us, to like us. These are the dynamic characteristics of The Wanter. It's so intense, so compelling, so believable. Most of the time, we get captured by it, and we believe this is all we are.

A lot of the human behaviors that have historically happened on Earth—and are still happening—are coming from people who are captured in their Wanter. But let's not villainize The Wanter. It's not the villain in this story. It's simply oriented in this way to ensure our survival.

We can start to understand this.

In my journey, I've been invited into natural ways of chanting, meditation, and ancient practices. There are natural ways that help us untangle from being so captured in The Wanter. Chanting is one of those ways. It energetically aligns the systems within the body, opening us to experience a deeper truth—an opening into the love that we are.

There are practices that I share, like: Name That Thought Practice, Problem Solver Mind Practice, First Growl Practice, the Living Practice, the Loving Blessing Practice, and of course, the chanting. Practices like *Madhya Vikasa, Viveka, Seva, Shiva Bhavana*. These are all ways I've found to be beneficial for myself and for others I've shared them with.

Many of these practices I learned at the ashram. Some of them came to me more organically—combinations of what I learned from my mom about really facing our feelings, which led to the Living Practice. Name That Thought Practice emerged out of the Cat-Mouse Meditation I learned at the ashram. The Loving Blessing Practice is exactly as I learned it there. The chanting, *Madhya Vikasa*, I learned both at the ashram. *Viveka* I learned at the ashram. *Seva* I learned at the ashram. *Shiva Bhavana*, I learned at the ashram.

There's a deep gratitude I have for all the wonderful ways I was invited to directly experience that I am the love I was looking for. This is what's inevitable in this class—this life— out here on the edge of the galaxy, in this solar system, in this advanced course I like to call Wanter Dynamics.

It reminds me of my days studying physics in my previous life as an engineer. We studied what were called field dynamics —the dynamic characteristics of energy fields. Electromagnetic energy fields were one of the areas I focused on. I became an engineer in that world: studied radio wave technology. We studied how energy fields orient themselves and interact. That was called electromagnetic field dynamics.

In the same way, we—these advanced students on planet Earth—are studying the dynamic characteristics of The Wanter.

And the practices, if we engage them regularly, allow us to become more stabilized in the direct experience that the love we are is eternal. It's what we have always been. We never actually separated from it. It has always been right here.

We are the love we've been looking for.

In this class I am calling Wanter Dynamics, we can involve ourselves in practices that allow us to directly experience the love we are. We become more stabilized, more established in that truth. We begin to live life more and more from that truth. Then we can honor and love our Wanter.

The war can be over–against our Wanter, and against everyone else when they're in their Wanter. We can love. We can play. We can share what we've found beneficial—if they're interested. We would never want to push any of this on anyone. We don't need to chase anyone down or force them to learn it. That's not the natural way. But if someone is interested, if someone wants to explore more deeply, we can share what we've noticed. Which is what we will be doing in this book

I humbly offer this as an invitation. May it serve you in the ways it has so beautifully served me. All I know for sure is that I love you all. I love you all with all my heart.

Welcome to Wanter Dynamics. And may you directly experience the love you are in the most pure and beneficial way.

THE WANTER

IMAGINE A LITTLE HUMAN FETUS IN THE WOMB OF ITS MOTHER. Imagine the conditions. It's nice and warm. All the needs are being met—nutrition, hydration, and oxygenated blood through the placenta. It's nice and cozy and warm there. All the needs are being met.

Eventually, after the development of this fetus into a little human baby, there will be the exiting of the womb—whether that happens through a natural birth or a C-section. Either way, there will be the exiting of the womb.

The instant this happens—there will now be a need for a new way of getting oxygen. The first breath will need to happen. There's going to be a new need that arises. One that wasn't occurring before in the womb, where oxygen was automatically provided through the oxygenated blood in the placenta. Now there's going to be a need for oxygen in a new way. There will have to be that first breath. I say that this is the moment a part of human consciousness that I call *The Wanter,* comes into service, to help get that need met.

This aspect of human consciousness that I call The Wanter, arrives to get that need met. Once the first breath happens, from that point on, The Wanter will have to try to ensure that there will continue to be oxygen. If we're underwater for some amount of time, there will come a point where The Wanter will start rising up and saying, "That's long enough. Get back up above the surface. We need some oxygen." If we're in some sort of situation where we're not getting oxygen, The Wanter will do whatever it takes to try to get that oxygen.

Now, after that need is met—let's say oxygen is now happening—the next need that's going to arise for this human infant is the need for warmth, because the human baby will be cold. It's not well suited for the environment. The human baby isn't born with a coat of fur to naturally insulate it and keep it warm; it's going to need a blanket. So The Wanter will need to call out for help when there's no language yet. *Wah wah wah.* What does The Wanter do when it needs help? It cries out for help, so there will be a signal to the other humans: *I need help.*

Let's say the baby is wrapped in a blanket. The Wanter will temporarily rest because the warmth need is now being met. But let's say that the blanket is removed for some reason—The Wanter will rise up again. *Wah, I'm cold. I'm cold.* Every time the body gets cold, The Wanter is going to need to rise up and try to fix that situation, solve that problem.

Let's say the body gets too hot—The Wanter will rise up and try to adjust that, try to find a cooler temperature. The Wanter has to want warmth every time we get cold. It can't just want warmth once. It has to want warmth *every* time.

The nature of this Wanter, this human expression aspect, is that it has to want oxygen every time, and it has to want warmth every time we get cold—or want a cooler temperature every time we get hot.

The next two primal needs are nourishment and hydration. Luckily, through breastfeeding, the human infant can get both of those needs met. Both nourishment and hydration can be met through breast milk. So every time the infant gets hungry or thirsty, the crying is a signal: *I need help.* Let's say the breast-feeding happens—The Wanter temporarily rests.

The nature of this aspect of human consciousness is that it's there for us—for survival—to make sure we have oxygen, the right temperature, nourishment, and hydration. Every time any one of those four things is needed, The Wanter will cry out. It will develop some sort of strategy to try to get those needs met. Then, when the needs are met, it will temporarily rest. But it will need to rise up again and get those needs met, and then it will temporarily rest, and then it will need to rise up again—and again.

The nature of this aspect of human consciousness that I call The Wanter is: to want. To use a strategy to try to get that need met—and then to want; to use a strategy to try to get that need met—and then to want. When it temporarily rests, that's what The Wanter calls happiness. When all the needs are met, The Wanter would say, *I'm so happy.* But it isn't really happiness—it's just that The Wanter has temporarily stopped wanting.

As life continues and the human infant starts to develop and become a toddler, there's now language, and there's going off to preschool, and all the things that happen in a life—The Wanter will still be in play. It will extend itself beyond the four primary needs: oxygen, right temperature, nutrition, and hydration.

Imagine a little toddler at preschool, and the little boy or girl sees a toy across the room that they want. Their Wanter will rise up and say, "I want that toy." Maybe the teacher says, "No, you can't have that toy."

"You don't understand, it's life or death. I have to have that toy—life or death." Their Wanter will do whatever it takes to get that toy.

Let's say that strategy worked and they got the toy—then their Wanter would say, "I'm so happy." If this were true happiness, all they'd ever need is that one toy. But it's not really happiness; it's just that The Wanter has temporarily stopped wanting. As soon as they look around and see that somebody else on the other side of the room has an even cooler toy, The Wanter will shift. The nature of The Wanter is to want. It will see that cooler toy and think, "No, not this toy. I want *that* toy. *That* toy." It's life or death. I have to have that toy. Their Wanter will come up with some sort of strategy to get the toy. If that strategy works, and they get the toy, their Wanter will say, "I'm so happy." But it's not true happiness. It's just that The Wanter has temporarily stopped wanting because The Wanter will then want again and again and again.

The Wanter will now be walking through the neighborhood and see that somebody's riding a bicycle. "I want a bicycle. It's life or death." They will come up with a strategy to get that bike. Let's say they get the bike. For a little bit, they'll be happy, they'll ride on their bike, and they'll be so happy that they've got their bike and they're riding their bike. But as soon as their wanter sees that somebody has an even cooler bike with special handlebars and a banana seat, The Wanter will say, "I want the special handlebars and the banana seat." Strategy, strategy, strategy to try to get that met. Let's say they get the special handlebars and the banana seat. They'll be what they'll call "happy," temporarily. But as soon as the next want comes online, The Wanter will want again. Now, instead of the bike, they'll want the car. "I want a fancier car. A nicer car. I want two cars. I want three cars. I want a house. I want more money. I want the right relationship. I want the attention. I want love. I want the right weather."

This Wanter aspect of human consciousness, its nature, will always be to want more. It's insatiable. It can't ever reach a true state of contentment, because by its very nature, it has to keep wanting. Many of our human interactions come from this aspect of human consciousness, where we're always wanting the next thing, with the idea that if I get *that*, then I'll be happy.

If I get *that*, then I'll be content. If I get *that*, then I'll be safe. If I get *that*, then I'll be secure . . . then I'll be content. If I get *that*, then I'll be fulfilled.

This plays out a lot in our human interactions with other people and with the living of life. Now, if we're ruled by our Wanter, we're always going to be searching for the next thing, with the idea that it will bring whatever it is we're looking for— whether it's happiness, contentment, fulfillment, safety, or security. The Wanter will always need more. It's insatiable. What each person's Wanter does is start developing a strategy, a system for getting what we want. A way to manipulate, control, and obtain what we desire. I call that aspect of the Wanter "*The* Solution." The Wanter creates *the* solution– coming up with a way to navigate life and get what you want–with the idea that it will bring you fulfillment. Now, each person has their own unique "The Solution," based on whatever trial-and-error methods seem to work to manage this place. Everybody has a different "The Solution."

This is why, when other people annoy us, the reason they are annoying us is that they're not doing it per our "The Solution." "The Solution" that *our* Wanter has created. And the reason they're not doing it per our "The Solution" is because they have their own unique "The Solution." They are not doing it right. And the reason they're not doing it per our "The Solution" is because they have their own unique "The Solution."

Everybody thinks their solution is "*The* Solution." Notice how I don't call it "A Solution." It's not optional; it's "*The* Solution." This is why other people annoy us. If you reflect for a moment and notice everyone you've ever known, there's been at least one thing they did that annoyed you. Even if it was just a mild annoyance, there's something they did that annoyed you. The reason it annoyed you is because they're not doing it per your "The Solution." Everyone you've ever known will have at least once annoyed you, and usually much more than just mild annoyance.

Our Wanter starts creating a grievance list against all the people we've interacted with. The people you've known longest have the longest grievance list—the ones your Wanter has known longer. Our core family members have the longest grievance list. Anybody we've just met might only have one or two grievances on our Wanter's Grievance List, where they didn't do it per our "The Solution." This is where grudges come from, and resentment, because they're not doing it right. They're not doing it per our "The Solution." What we start to notice is that everyone we've ever known—this dynamic—is playing out within our Wanter. Our Wanter has a grievance list on everybody and is at least mildly annoyed at everyone.

The other thing to realize is that this means everyone who has known us also has a grievance list on us. Everyone you've ever known, you have at least once mildly annoyed them— probably way more than that. There is no way you could do it per their "The Solution" everytime. You don't have their "The Solution." You have your Wanter's "The Solution." No matter how much we try to read people and morph ourselves just right to get them to like us, it turns out they don't actually unconditionally love us from their Wanter. The Wanter isn't capable of unconditional love. The Wanter does a *version* of love, but it has conditions. It will give what it calls love, as long as the person is compliant and is how The Wanter wants them to be. The Wanter can't love unconditionally. The Wanter can't even *like* unconditionally. It's not possible. All of our Wanters will always have conditions. This is why, when people start to annoy us, we will remove our love. Because it's not the real love. We will remove our like, because the Wanter can't do real like, can't do real love.

But the great news in this is that it's a part of our human expression. It's not the enemy. The Wanter is not the enemy. It's very much there to help us survive, to make things better for us. The Wanter, that's its whole function—to keep us alive. It's not the enemy. We don't want to in any way vilify the Wanter. It's there to help us. It just simply is trying to make things better for us.

Each of our Wanters is very selfish. By its very nature, it *has* to be selfish. It only cares about us. The Wanter only cares about its own self. Our Wanter doesn't care about other people. The Wanter can be very selfish, very manipulative, very controlling. It can be mean, hurtful, because the Wanter doesn't care about how it affects other people. Our Wanter only cares about how to make it better for us.

Let's say you're getting ready to go on a trip and you're about to get on the highway. You go up the on-ramp, and as you're about to pull into the highway, it's bumper-to-bumper traffic. It's very likely that your Wanter will be upset about that. The Wanter would want there to be no traffic for you, of course. But notice, at that moment, your Wanter isn't upset that there's traffic for everybody else. Your Wanter is only upset that there's traffic for *you*. Our Wanter only cares about us.

Any moment where we've been selfish, unkind, uncaring, mean, manipulative, or controlling—that's a moment where we've been trapped by our Wanter. We're just interacting with others from our Wanter. What this reveals to us is that anytime anybody has ever been unkind to us, if they've been controlling, manipulative, unkind, or not loving, it's because they're in their Wanter.

Once we start to realize this, we can start to see the human dynamic that plays out. In most human interactions we do tend to get pulled into our Wanter. The more stressful the situation, the more likely we are to get pulled into our Wanter, because the Wanter's job is to make it better for us. Our Wanter doesn't care about anybody else. Our Wanter only cares about us. If we're in our Wanter, we're going to do selfish things. Once again, it's not the enemy. It's not wrong or bad that this happens. It's needed for survival, the primary needs. The Wanter will extend beyond the four primary needs and start trying to manipulate and control the rest of life. This plays itself out.

The wonderful news is that once we start to notice this, The Wanter isn't all that we are. That's part of our human expression. What we also ultimately are is our spirit, our essence, and our true self. That eternal essence isn't a physical thing. That's why we use words like spirit, soul, essence, awareness, or presence. That aspect of our being is real. It's not a physical thing, and it's inherently kind, compassionate, caring, understanding, and patient. That is our True Nature. Our True Nature is inherently wise, loving, and capable of navigating life from a very wise perspective.

But there's also our Wanter.

This whole world that we're all experiencing together is a very dynamic play of whether we're in our Wanter or in our True Nature. The spiritual journey is about realizing *this*—about untangling from the tendency to interact with others from our Wanter, and being more likely to find natural ways to rest into our True Nature, and interact from there.

This is the dynamic play that we're all experiencing together, and what I call The Wanter and True Nature isn't like an on-off switch. It's not binary. It's on a continuum. We're either way in our Wanter or more in our True Nature. If we're all the way in our Wanter, then we're going to be completely selfish, mean, controlling, unkind, and not caring about others. If we're all the way in True Nature, we're going to be inherently loving, kind, patient, understanding, wise, capable, not a doormat, able to speak up, able to say no to things, and be able to navigate life in a very balanced and natural way. It's on a continuum. So, we might be partly in our Wanter in certain moments and more and more in True Nature in others.

There are lots of ancient practices that give us a chance to untangle from the tendency to get pulled into our Wanter and become more available to the experience of our True Nature. This is the lovely possibility of the reality we're all experiencing together—this dynamic play of the aspects within us: The Wanter and our True Nature.

In the coming chapters, we'll continue to explore this dynamic—this ongoing movement between The Wanter and our True Nature. We'll look at how it plays out in the everyday, and how easy it can be to get caught in it without even realizing we've been pulled in. We'll then explore some of the ancient practices that give us the chance to pause, notice, and rest back into something deeper. Not to fight or vilify The Wanter. Not to make it wrong. But to begin to recognize it, and from that recognition, begin to open ever more into our True Nature.

EMOTIONAL DISTURBANCE ORIGINS

LET'S TALK ABOUT EMOTIONS. WE, IN OUR HUMAN EXPERIENCE, have strong emotions, things like annoyance, frustration, anger, resentment, disappointment, dissatisfaction, sadness, loneliness, and depression. Yes, we have many strong emotions.

Where do these originate? What is the origin of these strong emotions? It's that aspect of our human consciousness called The Wanter, which is there within each of us to ensure our survival. It's that part of us that moves us from the cold back into the house where it's warm. That's the job of The Wanter—to help us survive. If we get cold, The Wanter will seek warmer temperatures for survival. The cold doesn't feel good. It's a disturbance, it's uncomfortable. The Wanter will always try to move away from discomfort and the feelings that don't feel good. The Wanter will always try to find some way to move toward something that would bring comfort when something uncomfortable is occurring. That aspect of us, for survival, leads us to venture out of the cave where the fire is, and when it's cold out there, that's uncomfortable. The Wanter is the part of us that will move us back into the cave where it's warm. If we get too hot, The Wanter will try to seek a cooler temperature because that heat is uncomfortable.

The nature of The Wanter is to always try to find comfort in the experience of discomfort, for survival reasons. So anytime we're having a disturbance, it's because something is occurring that The Wanter doesn't want to be happening.

Let's say we get annoyed. That's coming from our Wanter wanting something to be different than it is. When something's happening that isn't going how we want it to go, it can create a strong emotional response from our Wanter. All of these strong emotions are coming from our Wanter, that part of us that's always trying to make things ideal for us, better for us, comfortable for us.

Let's use the traffic example. Let's say you're going to go on a drive on the highway, and you go up the on-ramp to get on the highway, and you notice it's bumper-to-bumper traffic. There's likely to be some sort of response, and annoyance or frustration could even lead to an anger response. *Argh, fricking traffic.*

So where's that coming from? That's coming from our Wanter wanting something to be different than it is. This is a real obvious example. You come up the on-ramp, bumper-to-bumper traffic, and your Wanter wants there to be no traffic. The Wanter gets frustrated about that. It's wanting there to be no traffic. Again, notice your Wanter isn't upset that there's traffic for everybody else. Your Wanter is only upset that there's traffic for you. Each of our Wanters is selfish. It's looking out for what's best for us in that moment. Notice you've never been frustrated that there's traffic for everybody else. Your Wanter is upset that there's traffic for you.

Why? Because your Wanter's job is to seek out comfort. It's not going to be comfortable for The Wanter to have to sit in that bumper-to-bumper traffic and then be late to wherever we were headed. All those things are our Wanters wanting that situation to be different than it is. That creates the annoyance that's generated from The Wanter wanting there to be no traffic in that moment. That's where the disturbance is coming from.

Every disturbance that we have, whatever strong emotion, whether it's annoyance, frustration, anger, resentment, regret, heartbreak, loneliness, sadness, or fear, all the strong emotions, are coming from whatever's occurring, when our Wanter is wanting it to be different than it is. We're wanting that person to be different toward us. We're wanting that traffic situation to be different. We're wanting the weather to be different. We're wanting the situation to be different. We're wanting and wanting and wanting. Remember, the nature of The Wanter is that it will always be wanting something, using a strategy to try to get that in place, and then when the desire to change rises up again, it'll want to change again.

So every time we go up into bumper-to-bumper traffic, our Wanter is going to potentially have a response of wanting there to be no traffic. Why? Because it would be way better for us if there weren't any traffic. So The Wanter wants there to be no traffic. That's what creates that growl. I sometimes call it the growl. That first growl when something's not going how we want it, that can rise up in us, and then we might say or do something to try to change that situation. We might yell at the traffic; or we might say, "All these people, how come there has to be this traffic?"

If we get pulled into that, then how we experience the traffic is from that disturbance of wanting it to be different than it is and not getting what we want. Every interaction we have with another person, if they're annoying us in any way whatsoever, it is because we're wanting them to do it differently than they're doing it.

Notice, anytime you're ever annoyed at anyone, the reason you're annoyed is they're not doing it right. They're not doing it how *your* Wanter would do it. They're doing it how *their* Wanter would do it. This is why we get annoyed at other people.

They're not complying with how we want them to be doing it. Then we have a disturbance, and we might use some strategy to try to get them to do it how we want them to do it. We might say something to them from our disturbance: "How come you're doing that? I don't like that." Our Wanter will want things to be different, and that's what creates the disturbance.

Now, what we can also realize is this doesn't mean that our Wanter is not seeing things accurately. If we go back to the traffic example, The Wanter is very much seeing that situation accurately. The Wanter is right! It would be wonderful if there weren't any traffic. We're not saying The Wanter doesn't see things accurately. It very often does. When someone is being mean to us and The Wanter is upset about it, The Wanter is seeing it correctly. It's not lovely for them to say or do mean things to us. Of course, our Wanter would want them to not be doing that. The Wanter is seeing it accurately. The difference is, if we navigate it from our Wanter, then we're navigating it from the disturbance. If we get trapped in the disturbance of our Wanter, then how we navigate that moment is coming from that frustration, from that annoyance.

There's a chance that when we have a disturbance, any disturbance, we can just notice it, and stop to ask, "What is my Wanter wanting that it's not getting?"

"It's wanting that person to stop being mean to me."

How might we navigate this from wisdom, from our True Nature, our true self, from a larger perspective? If we always navigate from our Wanter, then we're just going to keep doing certain behaviors toward other people to try to control them, to try to get them to be different, to get them to do what we want. We might yell at them. We might raise our voice. We might try to harm them to get them to stop. We might try to guilt them. Our Wanter will try all kinds of things to get what we want.

The chance is, when we have some disturbance, to stop and just ask, "What is my Wanter wanting that it's not getting?"

"Oh, thank you, Wanter, for wanting that. You're right, it'd be way better for us if there wasn't traffic. Thank you so much. But I just need to let you know we don't have any control over that."

Then, we rest back in our true self, our peaceful self, our calm self, and then we experience the traffic from calm peacefulness rather than irritated, frustrated Wanter energy, the whole time we're in the traffic. From there, we might have clarity. When we're in our True Nature, we might realize, "I can put on a song that I like while I'm in the traffic." We might even have a wisdom that comes in as an insight: "You know what? That next exit, I think there's a back way. I think I'll get off at that next exit and see if I can find that back way to where I'm going."

We might notice there's all kinds of options for how we experience the moment, rather than habitually experiencing it from our Wanter, where we're frustrated, annoyed, trying to manipulate, and control. We can thank our Wanter because, very often, The Wanter is seeing the situation accurately. That's why it's wanting it to be different, because it's accurate. It'd be way better if it wasn't raining when we're having our picnic. Wouldn't that be great?

"Thank you so much, Wanter, for wanting it to be not raining when we're having our picnic. Let me see what my options are. Let's explore what our options are." We can navigate it from a more wise, larger perspective of our true self.

And so, every disturbance, we can start to notice, is coming from our Wanter wanting something that it's not getting.

Now let's explore what happens when we aren't able to catch it early and we get pulled into a disturbance. At that point, once we're fully affected and pulled into a disturbance, the best way that I have found over my years of exploring this is a practice I call the Living Practice, which we will dive deeper into in the coming chapters. In that practice, we have to be willing to turn toward the disturbance because now we're affected. We are pulled in and, at this point, The Wanter, of course, is going to try to distract us, find something else to do, numb out with alcohol, drugs, and all kinds of strategies that the Wanter will use to not have to face the disturbance.

The only way is to be willing to turn toward it, rather than moving away from it. At that point, it's essential to be willing to stop and just fully feel the disturbance. Notice where you're feeling it in your body, and allow it to be directly experienced. If you find yourself in a strong flow of disturbance, there are recordings included with this book that you can listen to—offered as a support to help you gently turn toward the feeling and stay with it, just as it is. These recordings are there to walk with you through the process of allowing the disturbance to be directly experienced, without needing to solve it, fix it, change it, or push it away. Then the energy can begin to move. It can be honored, felt, and allowed.

In the Living Practice, once you've let yourself fully feel the emotion—without trying to fix it—the next phase is simply to recognize it, not deny it or avoid it. The feeling is real, but it isn't the whole of who you are. You are also the awareness in which that disturbance appears.

Once we start including that, then the disturbance will start un-contracting all on its own. We don't have to do any sort of releasing; it just happens, by being willing to feel it, while also remembering that we're also the awareness of the feeling, honoring it, and allowing it to be as it is. Those contracted energies will, on their own, tend to release. As I say, the nuances of this practice are in the recording included in the book called the Living Practice.

WELCOME TO THIS DYNAMIC PLAY
OF PERSPECTIVES

WELCOME TO WHAT I REFER TO AS THE DYNAMIC PLAY OF perspectives. In our human lives, we will at some point begin to notice: this dynamic play of perspectives is always going on, in every moment. Whatever is occurring, is whatever is occurring. The occurrence is the occurrence. It could be a rainstorm on our picnic. It could be that the picnic is going so lovely and there is a beautiful sunset. There is a wide variety of the types of experiences we have in our lived human lives.

What we also begin to notice is: all of those experiences are temporary. All of those occurrences have a beginning, a duration, and a completion. Everything will have that vibrational flow—beginning, duration, completion—and whatever it is that is occurring, that will be the Truth. It will have a beginning, duration, and completion. A beginning, middle, and end.

While that's occurring, whatever perspective we are in determines what it's like for us to be in that experience. So in this play, this dynamic play of perspectives, if we are all the way in that which I call The Wanter, then whatever is occurring, we are going to experience from the perspective of needing to have control of it, to manage it. That it's a problem. "How do we get it to be better? How do we change this?" To resist it. "I don't like this. I don't want this rain happening on my picnic."

If we are all the way in True Nature, the other end of this dynamic play of perspectives, we are then in acceptance, and we are experiencing it as the adventure it is. So that same occurrence—the rain that is now raining on our picnic—is experienced from the perspective of acceptance. That experience can now become an adventure.

Maybe we end up having a "Let's dance in the rain" experience. It is a possibility. That same occurrence—the rain that is now happening on our picnic that we planned for three weeks, we were so excited to have this wonderful picnic with our friend in the park, and then it began raining—that is going to be temporary. It will have a beginning, duration, and completion. That same event can be experienced on that continuum of perspectives—all the way in The Wanter, or all the way in True Nature, or somewhere in between, a combination. It is a variable scale.

If we are all the way in our Wanter, we are going to be mad, and hating it, and against it, and feeling like it is so unfair. If we are all the way in True Nature, we will have a dance party in the rain. We might even sing songs—rain songs. We might dance or celebrate, and we wonder what it's like to dance in the rain on top of our wet picnic blanket. All possibilities are open to us when we are in the perspective of acceptance—in the reveal of Oneness—as compared to the conceal of Oneness.

There are various ways of referring to this dynamic play of perspectives. When we are all the way in The Wanter, that is where we resist. We are in the forgetting. Everything is a problem. We are trying to control and manipulate and manage. We get overwhelmed. There is lots of suffering. If we are all the way in True Nature, in the reveal, it's an adventure. We are in acceptance. We don't have a problem here. "Let's dance in the rain."

This is the dynamic play of perspectives, in which all of

life's temporary occurrences are experienced—somewhere on that continuum of the dynamic play of perspectives. It isn't wrong or bad if we do get pulled into the conceal—the forgetting perspective, the resisting, the play of The Wanter. That isn't wrong or bad when that happens. We're exploring what that's like. Each moment in life gives us the opportunity to explore this play of perspectives.

It is very dynamic, and there will be times where we get pulled into the resisting. Then we get to experience the suffering that comes with that. That is not wrong or bad; it is just another way of experiencing that moment.

Now, what tends to happen is the more we become aware of this, we tend to experience more and more from the larger perspective of wholeness, of the adventure of it all. Beginnings, durations, completions. Beginnings, middles, endings. And our perspective of those three events—either from the perspective of The Wanter, or from True Nature. That just inevitably happens. But, even if we do get pulled in, that's part of this lived human experience. There will always be this dynamic play of perspectives.

Welcome to the wild and lovely adventure of human life!

ACCEPT OR SUFFER

IN THESE LIVES THAT WE'RE LIVING HERE, WE BEGIN TO NOTICE that in every moment we have a choice. We can either accept what's occurring, or we can resist what's occurring. When we resist, it creates suffering—what we might call psychological suffering, emotional suffering—and we resist. Through the years, I've often said that in every moment we can either accept or suffer, because if we resist, that pulls us into the suffering. If we're accepting what is, there's no suffering in acceptance. Then we can actively navigate whatever's occurring from true acceptance.

This teaching has been offered up by anyone who has really started to take a look at the nature of human life. It's been offered up through the ages by various explorers of the nature of human expression. In every moment, we can either be accepting what's occurring or resisting what's occurring.

I'm going to offer a metaphoric story that gives an example of how you actually navigate life from acceptance. What might that even look like? In this story, the setting will be a jungle, which represents life on Earth. We're all in this jungle. There are three different people in the jungle, and these three different people are going to represent the three different versions of us in every moment. We can be one of these three or some sort of combination thereof.

The first person in our story is somebody who always resists what is. They never accept. They're in that part of being called The Wanter—that part of us that wants things to be different, with the idea that if I could just get things how I want them to be, then I'll be okay. That is the part of us that's always trying to manipulate and control and get what we want, with the idea that it will bring us happiness. The first person is someone who's always in that way of orientation regarding life events— always in The Wanter, always resisting and trying to control and get things to be how they want them to be. That's one way that we can be in life.

The second person in our story will be somebody who has heard these teachings about acceptance and resistance—that in every moment, we can either accept or suffer. They've heard these teachings, but they don't fully understand them. They're not quite in full flow with it. They might have a bit of a misunderstanding regarding it. That'll be our second person in the jungle.

Our third person in the jungle is someone who has heard these teachings for many years and has lived them for decades. They're a veteran of this wisdom. From their direct experiences of their life journey, they've now arrived in this wisdom, and they navigate life from this perspective.

We have our three people in the jungle: The first person in the jungle—this is our person who's in The Wanter—is walking along, headed toward a destination, and they step in quicksand.

They might say, "Unbelievable! How come there has to be this quicksand? This is so unfair. Who's to blame? I hate when these things happen to me. This is so unfair!" This particular version of The Wanter has very much gotten pulled into the victim: *This shouldn't be happening to me.* They're wanting it to be different than it is. The whole time they're resisting and complaining about it, they just get swallowed up and they die in the quicksand. *Glub, glub, glub.*

Now we go to our second person in the jungle. This is someone who's heard these teachings, but they don't quite have a full understanding of it yet. This is, in many ways, the perspective of our mind. When our mind hears these teachings, our mind thinks that this is what it would mean to be in acceptance. Our second person's walking along in the jungle, headed toward a destination, and they step in quicksand.

"There's quicksand in my jungle. Well, I've heard the teachings that I can either accept or suffer; and if I resist, I'm going to suffer. I guess I don't want to resist this. I guess I just have to accept this quicksand. Hello, quicksand. I accept you just how you are." *Glub, glub, glub.* They die in the quicksand. Very passive. A doormat. That's not the true meaning of acceptance. Acceptance isn't passivity. This is the misunderstanding. When our mind hears these teachings, our mind often thinks, *If I accept everything, then I'll just get bowled over by everyone and have to go along.* That's not the true meaning of acceptance.

That leads us to our third person in the jungle, who has been living this for decades and decades. Here comes our third person, walking along in the jungle, headed toward a destination, and they step in quicksand.

"Oh wow, there's quicksand in my jungle. Okay, what are my options here? Because if at all possible, I would choose to get out of this quicksand." So the first thing they come up with to try is to call out for help. "Help! Somebody help! I'm in quicksand! Help!" They wait for a bit. "Help! I'm in quicksand! Help!" But there's nobody there for them. They accept that.

Then they might say, "Okay, nobody is there for me. What's my next option?" They look to their left and see that there's a tree with a low-hanging limb, and they wonder, if they lean over a little bit, if they could reach it. So they lean over as far as they can and try to reach the low-hanging limb, but it's out of reach. And they accept that. They say, "I can't reach it. Okay, what's my next option?"

Because they had leaned over for the tree limb that they weren't able to reach, they then noticed there's a little bit of solid land to their left—a bank of solid land. "Let's see what's up here." So they reach around on the solid land and find a rock. "No, that won't help me." They accept that. They put it down.

"What's my next option?" They keep looking on the bank and find a shell. "No, I can't see how that would help me." They accept that. "What's my next option?" They keep looking and find a twig. "Nope. I can't see how this would help me either." They put the twig down. "Okay, what's my next option?"

They keep looking and, as they reach a little bit further up, they say, "What is that? Is that a root of a tree, or is it a vine? It's a vine? Let me see if I can get my other hand on it." They reach over and get both hands on the vine, and they slowly pull themselves out of the quicksand.

Now that they're out of the quicksand, they look back at it and say, "Let me see if I can learn from this experience by seeing if I can tell the difference between quicksand and regular land."

They look at it from all different angles. It takes a little bit of time because it's very subtle. But after a while, looking at it from all those different angles, they start to notice: "It's a little lighter in color, a little different texture. That's what quicksand looks like. Maybe now I don't have to step in quicksand."

Now that our third person in the jungle knows what quicksand looks like. They decide, "Okay, lemme get some rocks." They gather up a bunch of rocks and start placing them all around the perimeter of that particular quicksand—mark it out and make it very noticeable where it is, so that they won't step in it anymore.

They continue on their journey. They didn't have one second of suffering over this event. They navigated it from active acceptance. They're the only one who got out of the quicksand, and they head on their journey toward their destination in the jungle.

If we take a look at what unfolded here, everything they tried that didn't work could have pulled them back into their Wanter. Like when they called out for help and there was nobody there. That could have pulled them back into their Wanter—could have created a whole story. "Of course nobody's there for me. I'm always there for everybody else, and the one time I need help, nobody's there for me."

But they didn't let that pull them into a story. That would have pulled them into their Wanter and created suffering. When there was nobody there for them, they just accepted it and explored, "What would be my next option?" Then they tried to reach the low-hanging limb, which they couldn't reach, and they simply accepted that. They didn't resist it. It didn't become an event that would pull them into their Wanter. Then they found the rock—and that didn't help them.

Each one of these things could have pulled them in. The rock could have become a story like this: "Of course I would find a rock—the one thing that'll just take me down even faster. Of course *I* would find a rock." No, they didn't get pulled into those kinds of stories.

Each thing that didn't work—they accepted it and explored the next option. The shell didn't work. The twig didn't work. Then when they found the vine, they pulled themselves out. Then, from active acceptance, they took time to see if they could learn from this event—to survey and take a close look at the quicksand. It turns out it was a little lighter in color, a little different texture. And they clearly marked it with rocks—from active acceptance. Then they were able to continue on their journey.

What we get to see is: in true acceptance, we're not passive. We're very active, and we explore our options. If we take a look at the third person in the jungle, what they were doing all along the way—each thing that they tried that didn't work—they were showing up for the lovely possibility that it *would* work. But they weren't attached to that outcome being the only way it could work.

They showed up for the lovely possibility that calling out for help would work. But it didn't work. That was the lovely possibility. Now, if they were attached to that outcome—and it *had* to work—then when it didn't work, that would have pulled them back into their Wanter. "This is so unfair! How come it didn't go how I wanted?"

But the way the third person is navigating the situation is: they're showing up for the lovely possibility without being attached to the outcome. Each thing they tried—that was the next lovely possibility. But they weren't attached to the outcome.

Because they weren't attached to the outcome, they were willing to show up for the next lovely possibility. When *that* didn't work, because they weren't attached, they were willing to show up for the *next* lovely possibility. Again and again until something did work. The third person in the jungle navigates life from active acceptance.

Active acceptance is not passive. We're able to keep exploring our options without being attached to the outcome. We just keep showing up for the lovely possibility—without being attached to the outcome. This is true acceptance—very active. We accept what is, and we navigate accordingly.

THE RETIRED AIRLINE CAPTAIN

LET'S EXPLORE WHAT IT'S LIKE TO NAVIGATE BEING WITH PEOPLE when they're really, really disconnected from their heart—really trapped in that aspect of the divine essence that I call The Wanter. Because when we're really captured in our Wanter, we can be quite wild, to say the least. We could even say: buck wild.

Sometimes we will be encountering people when they're in that very buck wild, very primal part of the divine essence that I call The Wanter. How might we navigate moments like that? Those can be quite tricky—it can get quite intense.

About eleven years ago, a woman that I had been sitting with for two years at that point had been dating someone—a retired airline captain—and I had been hearing about him in the explorations that I was having with her. One day, during a lunch break, my phone rings, and it's a number I didn't recognize, but I got the knowing that I should answer it. I did. It was him—the boyfriend, the retired airline captain. He was around sixty-nine or seventy at the time.

"Hi. So nice to speak with you," I said.

"I would like to schedule with you," he said.

I said, "Okay. I don't know if she happened to mention it to you, but I always invite people to allow three hours, at least, for our explorations."

Here's what I hear on the phone: "Three fucking hours? You gotta be kidding me."

There is a lot of information there. He's clearly not choosing this on his own. Because the next thing I hear on the phone—after he says that—is this: "Oh, okay, sure. Right. Yeah, that would be okay. Let's go ahead and schedule that."

You can imagine that she's in the room, and she's giving him *the* look, and he's now complying and saying that he's willing to go along with it, even though you can tell he doesn't want to. There's a lot of information in this initial phone call. We found the date and the time, and we scheduled it.

When the day arrived for him to be here at the studio I happened to be up front as he was walking up the sidewalk. I could see him walking toward the front door, and I was right there as he was walking in. I stood there and greeted him and said hello. He reached out his hand for a handshake—pretty aggressively. I remember thinking, "Oh, okay. Here we go."

I go in for the handshake, and as he grabs my hand, he is squeezing as hard as he can. You could tell he's trying to crush my bones in my hand. That's a tricky moment. That's a very aggressive Wanter. That's a real primal Wanter energy—very aggressive. Trying to assert dominance and crush my hand.

In that moment, there's a choice that I make. For years and years, this has been a way that has just unfolded for me—from seven years at the ashram, and four more years with eleven more teachers—learning all these really wonderful, natural ways of dropping into the heart and letting that be where we navigate life from.

In that moment, I just dropped, instantaneously—all that I Am, all my attention dropped into the very deepest heart essence within my being. *The Hṛdayam*, the Heart of Being, we would say in Sanskrit. The heart chakra. I drop in there, and I become aware of all the divine friends and my divine self. That Source Essence is always what we are in the very heart of being. So I drop in there—into the heart of being.

What I then inwardly say is, "Please let me be love. Please let me be love." In those moments, I'm aligning with love. "Please let whatever action happens now come from love." That happened instantaneously, as he's trying to crush my hand with all his strength.

All of a sudden, I could feel the muscles in my arm are now very strongly activated—and I'm now squeezing his hand back very firmly. It turns out, *that* was love. That's what love looked like. That's how the love that I am was expressed in that moment. It was a very firm squeeze, as I have a very strong grip. When you spend your whole life growing up as a baseball player, gripping a baseball bat your whole life, you develop a very strong grip. To his surprise—I have a very strong grip. That's what love looked like. *Please let me be love.* It was a very firm squeeze back. Just a little brief, firm squeeze. In that moment, if I could give words to the essence of that energy as I was squeezing his hand back, it was this: *Come on now, we can do better than this.* Another way to say it might be: *I love you too much to let you hurt me. I love you too much to let this happen. We're not going to do this to each other. We can do better than this.* All of that was the energy of that really firm, loving squeeze.

He backed off his grip and had a surprised look on his face. Then he let go. Now, moment to moment through this whole flow, I'm continuing to drop back into the heart of being. *Please let me be love.* Aligning with all that divinity that we are—the very heart essence, the revealed heart within us. There comes a point where the heart that we are is so revealed, we can navigate these tricky moments from there. *Please let me be love. Please let me be love.*

Then I'm dropping back into the heart after the firm

squeeze: *Come on now, we can do better than this. We're not going to hurt each other.* In many ways, that firm squeeze was actually an invitation for him to join me in this loving kindness.

Next, I say to him, "So, what's it like for you to be here today?"

He took that as if I were somehow attacking him, because here's what he said in reply: "What are you talking about? I don't do anything I don't want to do."

Oh. Okay. I dropped back into the heart. Now, I'm not taking this personally at all because I know who he really is. I'm resting in the heart with him. He is what I am. He is this love. He is this eternity. He is this divinity.

Now, he's not in touch with it. He's disconnected from it. And he's really in his Wanter, and his Wanter is being very aggressive. So we're getting a feel for how his Wanter is oriented. His Wanter is oriented very aggressively.

So with his response: "What are you talking about? I don't do anything I don't want to do." I dropped back into the heart. *Please let me be love.* Then this came out of me: "But really, what is it like for you to be here today?"

He said, "Something wrong with your ears? I just told you I don't do anything I don't want to do."

I dropped back into the heart again. *Please let me be love.*

"What would it be like for you in this moment just to be really honest with me?" I asked.

"What are you talking about?"

Dropped back into the heart.

"You know . . ." I said, "what would it be like for you right now just to let me have it?"

"Really?" he said.

I said, "Yeah, absolutely."

You could just see The Wanter get really aggressive and rise up. He got in a real aggressive stance, pointed his finger right in my face—and said, "I think you're full of shit."

It was so good. A whole belly laugh just came out of me, because he was finally being honest. I didn't mean to belly laugh. It just happened. It was so wonderfully lovely.

He got a really surprised look on his face when that happened.

He said, "That didn't bother you?"

I said, "No, not at all. Thank you so much for being so honest with me."

"What?" he said.

"I just want to thank you so much for being so honest with me," I said. "So, what's been going on?"

"Oh my God. Mitch—for two years, all I've been hearing, every time I do something she doesn't like, is: 'Mitch says this' and 'Mitch says that,' and 'How come you don't do it like Mitch says to do it?' and 'You need to talk to Mitch.' Mitch this and Mitch that—for two years. That's all I've been hearing. The only reason I'm even here is because she gave me an ultimatum. She told me if I didn't come to see you, she was going to break up with me."

I just looked at him and said, "Oh my goodness, I'm so sorry."

He softened into that a bit. He said, "Well, it's not your fault."

I said, "That's so kind of you to say. You know what? You don't have to be here today. You can turn around and head on out. You don't have to be here at all."

He softened even more as he looked around. "Well, this is a pretty cool place you've got here. What else have you got in this place?"

There was a giggle that came out. I said, "Would you like me to show you around?"

He said yes.

I said, "Well, first I'm going to invite you to take off your shoes."

"You want me to do what?"

"You know, it just keeps my place nice and clean. Would you be willing to do me that favor and remove your shoes?" I asked.

"Okay. I could see that," he said and sat down on the little bench that I have right there at the entryway, and he undid his lace shoes, and then we had a tour.

I'm not going to stop and show him certain things that would just confuse him and make him wonder, *Who is this guy?* Like my *puja* to my Guru in India. I'm not going to show him any of that stuff—it would just confuse him and wouldn't be useful to him at all.

So we had an abbreviated tour. We sat down in the chairs. I served him some tea, and I'm just loving him. I'm just honoring him. I'm just letting him be right where he is on the journey. I don't have any agenda. I don't need to fix him. I don't need to change him. I don't need to solve him. I don't need to analyze him. I don't need to extract anything from him. I don't need anything—because I know who he really is. I'm resting in that with him. I'm resting in his True Nature, which is also my True Nature. It is all of our True Nature—our divine essence.

As I'm resting there with him, he starts telling me about how he recently retired after many years as an airline captain. That was fun for me because, earlier in life, I was on a similar path. I'd flown airplanes in college, earned my private, commercial, and instrument ratings, and became a flight instructor. So I was really enjoying listening to him share about his flying career. I wasn't doing anything except being there with him—fully present, honoring him, allowing him to be seen and heard just as he is. No agenda. Just companioning him as he shared his journey.

He could tell by some of my responses to his sharing of his career as an airline pilot that I know a bit about aviation. He asked me, "You seem to know about aviation. Do you have any connection to that?"

I said, "Well, yes—nothing like what you've done with your career. But I did. When I first went to college, I did fly airplanes. At one point, I thought I was going to be an airline pilot."

"Where did you go to school?" he asked.

I knew that he would know Embry-Riddle Aeronautical University. So you don't have to say the whole thing, because everybody in that world—anybody in aeronautical science, whether it's aviation or space—everybody knows about Embry-Riddle Aeronautical University. It's one of the best schools in the country, probably the world, for that field.

So I said, "Well, I went to Embry-Riddle."

He looked at me and said, "*You* went to Embry-Riddle?" His Wanter started coming out again—very skeptical.

"Yes, I went to Embry-Riddle."

He said, "Tell me about Embry-Riddle."

You can tell he's wanting something specific that only somebody who actually went there would know. So I told him a few things. Something that only people who went there would know is that the airplanes have the N-number with an *ER* on the end of it. Every airplane has what's called its N-number—its identification number. It's the letter 'N,' then several numbers, and then some letter designators. In the aviation world, you don't say 'A, B, C, D, E, F, G—'there's a whole pilot alphabet: Alpha, Bravo, Charlie, Delta, Echo, etc.

Every airplane at Embry-Riddle has its number and then *ER*, which would be 'Echo Romeo.' I shared all that with him.

He said, "Oh, so you really did go to Embry-Riddle?"

I said, "Yes, I did. I'll only tell you the truth. I won't make things up. I'll just share with you from my direct experience."

"What did you do after Embry-Riddle?" he asked.

I said, "I worked on the space shuttle program at the Kennedy Space Center."

"You worked at the Kennedy Space Center on the space shuttle program?"

"Yes, I did."

Then he asked for more details, so I shared some insider things—like how you have to wear bunny suits in the clean rooms. When you're inside the orbiter, the bunny suit is necessary because anything loose—like eyelashes—needs to be contained. There's a whole process: you go through an air shower, put on the suit, then go through another air shower. I walked him through the whole flow. I also talked about the Hubble Space Telescope I worked on, the Galileo probe, and other details only someone who worked on those projects would know. He found it all really fascinating.

For two and a half hours, we explored those things together —and he didn't even want to be here at all.

Suddenly, I could feel a shift happen for him, and his hand went to his chest. You could feel that he was having a heart opening. He got real tender and, with his hand on his chest, he said, "Mitch, this is really weird. I'm having a swirling energy in my chest." His heart was opening.

I said, "Would it be okay if you just close your eyes and let yourself be available to this?"

He turned his head kind of sideways and said, "I guess that would be okay."

"Thank you," I said.

He closed his eyes, and as soon as he did, you could tell he was going through something very intense. Some tears started to come, and he wiped them really quickly so that I wouldn't see them. You could see there were intense energies going on in his body. A few more tears came, and he wiped them as quickly as possible. I'm just being with him. I'm just honoring, just resting in the loving acceptance with him. A very intense flow happened, and he started sobbing and sobbing and sobbing—the kind of sob where you're just completely captured in it. He was heaving and sobbing, in a really intense flow. I'm just being with him. I'm just companioning him. I'm just resting in his True Nature with him—loving him, honoring him, accepting him, being with him. I'm just honoring him as he is, allowing him to be as he is.

For about forty-five minutes, it flowed like that. It would sometimes be less intense, and he'd blow his nose, and it would happen again and again like that—in waves and waves and waves. Very intense, but it got less and less, and it was releasing and releasing as I was being with him and honoring him and allowing him to be as he is.

Because I know who he really is. He is what I am, what you are, what we all are. He is a divine being, having this temporary human experience. He is divine essence, experiencing this vibration, which is also the divine essence—this intense energy that he's also experiencing. Whatever frequency or intensity of energy it is, it's all the divine essence, always—expressing itself as various frequencies in temporary waves.

As it eventually moved and flowed its way all the way through. He opened his eyes and blew his nose again.

He looked at me and said, "Wow."

I said, "Yeah, wow. It was amazing to experience that with you."

He said, "Mitch, you're just so easy to talk to."

I said, "Oh, that's so kind of you to say."

He said, "I feel like I could tell you anything."

"Thank you for that. Is there something you're wanting to share?"

He looked at me, and you could see he was feeling so much love, so much gratitude. Then he glanced to his left and right, as if to make sure no one was about to overhear what he was about to say—which, of course, was funny, because we were inside the studio. But still, that's what he did. It was clearly something tender, something he felt vulnerable sharing.

He leaned forward in his chair, kind of in a whisper voice, and you could tell he was feeling so much gratitude and love for me. He was so grateful for what had just happened. He looked at me with such love and said, "Mitch, for the first time in my life, I've experienced what real love is." As soon as he said it, you could see—right as the words came out of his mouth— he realized that the love he was feeling toward me was also the love that he was. You could feel that he realized it as soon as he said it out loud. He gets that look of insight—that moment of clarity.

He said, "And you know what I just realized?"

"What?"

"It's also within me," he said.

I started sobbing when he said it—it was so tender and so beautiful. He started sobbing. We're two grown men sitting together in the heart of being, sobbing with gratitude for the potential of this liberation, of this love that we are. It was so wonderful, so simple, so natural, so lovely.

Then he took a big breath and said, "Mitch, I think that's enough for today."

"Absolutely," I said.

Then he paused for a moment, looked at me with such playfulness, and asked, "You got any openings next week?"

He and I have been exploring ever since.

We found out, as the next explorations unfolded, that he had a very intense childhood—a very domineering, abusive father—and nothing was ever good enough. He wasn't ever allowed to cry. When he got an A-minus instead of an A-plus, he got yelled and screamed at: "You're an idiot. What are you doing? You need to work harder." It was never enough. He had a rough go. The way his Wanter oriented itself to survive was to get aggressive—to fight against, to overtake, to dominate, to take charge. He learned it from his father. So that's the way he arrived with me that day. He arrived identified as that very aggressive Wanter, who had, for two years, been hearing about this guy Mitch, thrown in his face every time he did something his girlfriend's Wanter didn't like.

His Wanter wanted to come here and then be able to go back and tell her, "This guy's full of shit. Don't ever bring his name up to me again."

In that moment, when he squeezed my hand and I dropped into the heart of being—*please let me be love*—the way the love looked in that moment was a very firm squeeze back: *Come on now. We can do better than this. We're not going to hurt each other.*

Moment to moment, as I just kept aligning with love, the way the love looked in each moment was unique. That's a possibility when we're with people in very tricky Wanter situations—to drop into the heart of being and align with that love that we are. *Please let me be love. Please let me be love.* Then, whatever action or response comes from there—we let that be our compass. Moment to moment to moment.

As the years have gone on, he has shared, "That first day I got here, I didn't know what to do with you, because no matter how much I tried to provoke you and get you to fight me, it was like punching at air. There was nobody there to hit. I had never experienced what real love is. You were able to be loving and kind to me even when I was just being terribly mean to you." He often offers his gratitude and his apologies.

I always tell him, "You don't need to apologize. That's okay."

Now, he's at the point where there will be really tender moments where he'll say, "Mitch, I love you so much."

And I say to him, "I love you as well."

Isn't it wonderful that the love that we are can be liberated? That we can let the love we are be lived into the world? This is the lovely possibility. In any moment, in any tricky situation you find yourself in, there is a way to meet it from your True Nature. As we go further into the book, we'll explore practices that help build that momentum—practices that gently return us to presence, again and again—so that, moment to moment, we can let the choice be love.

When we let the choice be love, we are free. We can let that be our compass when navigating this very tricky land of The Wanter, in which everyone is a divine being—who mostly forgets that. Who mostly is not connected to that. They might mostly do Wanter-type behaviors to us. But, if we can rest in the heart of being, we won't take it personally. We'll be able to interact with them from this love that we are, which will look unique in every moment.

Sometimes, it might be a firm squeeze of the hand—that's pure love: *Come on now. I love you too much to let you hurt me.* Sometimes, it might be: *What's it like for you to be here?* Inviting. Letting him know that it's okay to let that part of him that's annoyed to be here, come out to play. Even at that point where what came out of me was, *What would it be like for you in this moment just to let me have it?* That's when he said, "I think you're full of shit."

When you're really resting in True Nature, you wouldn't take any of that personally. You'll be able to navigate it from this eternal, absolute, unharmable love that you are, and that you've always been, and that you will always be.

What we discover is: when we let the choice be love, we're home. We're free.

It's who we really are.

THE SHAKTI RIVER

WELCOME TO THIS *SHAKTI* RIVER. WHAT IS *SHAKTI*? *SHAKTI* IS A Sanskrit word. In its essence, it refers to the primordial cosmic energy. It's a way of speaking of the dynamic forces that move through the universe. It's the absolute source energy. *Shakti.*

In my years at the ashram, we would speak of the power of what we are—the power that permeates all existence—the source energy, the absolute source energy that has the ability to express itself in myriad subtleties and densities. This metaphor that I'm using—the *Shakti* River—is a way of referring to this primordial cosmic source energy that flows everywhere, every when, every every. All the time. The power that permeates all reality—the primordial cosmic energy—is the *Shakti*. We're always in that. We are that. We're all made of that. There's only that. This primordial source energy that's permeating all reality—we are always in the *Shakti* River. We are expressions of the *Shakti* River. You can't ever separate out from the flow. That's why I'm using the word river—this flowing source energy that I'm playfully referring to as the *Shakti* River. We're always that—everything, everyone, at all times.

Now, we have this ability, through the power of our attention, to shift our perspectives. If we're relaxing back into this larger perspective, we can have the direct experience of this primordial source energy—*Shakti*. It's in the direct experience that this inherent energy reveals itself. Otherwise, it's just a concept that our mind is creating from a description. As I'm describing this, your mind will be creating a concept. Now, if you've had the direct experience, your frame of reference will be different.

In the ancient traditions, the ancient lineages, there's always the invitation into practices—ways of shifting attention—so that we can have a direct experience of *Shakti* ourselves, of the primordial cosmic source energy that permeates all reality. That's how the Truth is revealed—in the direct experience. And the play is a play of perspectives, which are determined by where our attention is.

If our attention gets pulled into the limited thoughts and beliefs of our mind, into The Wanter—that part of our human expression that wants things to go a certain way and tries to control and manipulate reality to get it to be in some particular orientation that feels safe and secure and known—then that part of our human experience very naturally tries to control and bring things into a particular arrangement, a particular orientation, to feel safe and secure. This is why, whenever we're in situations that aren't familiar to us, that are unknown, risky, or potentially uncontrollable, it creates a disturbance in The Wanter, which likes things to be in control, known, safe, and secure. That's a part of our human expression that's necessary for our survival, as we've spoken of in previous chapters.

What we're now refining is this play of attention. If our attention is pulled into that perspective, then we see reality as something to be solved, a dilemma, a burden. Overwhelmed in that perspective, this is where we get pulled into the belief that the only way out is to die. This is where suicide comes from— the final conclusion of our Wanter. If it can't get things to be a certain way and it seems so hopeless—with no possibility—it can spiral itself down into its final conclusion: that the only way out of the pain is death.

That's one play—where the perspective is that this whole reality is a problem, a dilemma, and overwhelming. That's a very natural place that we get pulled into in our human experience. The lovely possibility is to realize that, while that's real and it is a part of our experience, it's not all that we are. Because there's a subtler essence to us—this awareness.

We use words like awareness. Notice how, right in this moment, there's the part of you that's aware of the words you're reading. Now, the part of you that's aware of these words isn't a physical thing. The reading of the words is happening through your eyes, which are part of your body, and there's all kinds of wiring inside the eyes to process that energy. Very similar to my first career—I was an engineer, and I worked in the field of electromagnetic and radio waves. The devices that we would create to transmit and receive information through the broadcast and reception of electromagnetic energy. This is how we navigate and communicate in that world when I used to work at the space center.

In the same way, if our attention gets pulled into that limited perspective, we can lose track of the awareness, the subtlety. The part of you that's aware of these words is not a physical thing. Notice how you couldn't grab hold of the awareness and show it to someone, and yet it's real. It's not made out of molecules. It's not made out of matter. It's a subtler dimension of existence that we sometimes call awareness.

Now, all of this—the awareness and the matter—are all flows of the *Shakti*, the primordial source energy. The *Shakti* is permeating all the subtleties, like awareness, and all the densities, like matter. The *Shakti* permeates all of it. It is a unifying essence, a source energy that permeates all reality. If our attention is resting back into the simplicity and the naturalness of presence, of awareness, we can start to experience that this awareness that we are isn't limited to our physical form.

Notice—the awareness that you are, that's aware of the words on the page, is also aware of your body. Your body exists and is real. It's a coalescing of *Shakti*. It's a congealing, a gathering of *Shakti* energy that we call a human body, that has all kinds of capacities to feel sensations, and have emotions and thoughts and beliefs and experiences. All of that is real—and temporary. Everything in the physical dimension of *Shakti*—the source energy—is a wave, a temporary wave. A wave that has a beginning, a duration, and then a completion. That's why the nature of the physical aspect of *Shakti* is temporariness. Everything has a beginning, a duration, and a completion.

The subtlety that we are—the awareness—isn't subject to those same parameters. The awareness that we are doesn't have beginnings and endings. It simply exists. It can't die. It can't even age. Notice—the awareness that you are, that's aware of these words, is the same awareness as it was ten minutes ago, ten days ago, ten years ago. It's the same awareness. Notice how it's still the same awareness. It can't age. It doesn't have molecules that can age. It's eternal. This awareness that you are will exist forever. You've always been this, and you will always be this.

Now, the human mind can't conceive of that. The human mind operates in linearity, logic, and reason. To the human mind, eternity isn't fathomable. It isn't logical that we exist forever. That truth is beyond the mind—and it's through the mind that we get pulled into The Wanter and its limited perspective.

This is all a play of perspectives. We're either in the perspective of The Wanter—where this whole reality is seen as a problem to be solved, controlled, and manipulated—or we rest our attention back into source energy, Source Essence, *Shakti*. We begin to experience that there's an essence we are—

this source energy—that we are, the *Shakti* that permeates all reality. This essence isn't at risk. It isn't affectable.

Notice how the awareness that you are can't be affected by the words you are reading. The awareness that you are can't be affected by anything. There is no life event you've ever experienced that has touched this presence—that you are this awareness, this eternal *Shakti*. Everything is always a varying expression of the *Shakti*—the power, the primordial cosmic energy. We're always in The *Shakti* River. We are expressions of it. This is where we're all connected and not separate. These aren't just "woo-woo" words. It's the Truth. It's directly experienceable.

In my previous career, we would do experiments and tests and verify things by trial and error—through cause and effect. In the same way, spiritual lineages have explored the nature of reality like inner-realm scientists—through practices, through shifting attention into the inner realm of existence, into the subtlety of being.

There are many practices. We will explore several of them in the coming chapters. There's the Name That Thought Practice, where we name the thought and rest back to see if another one comes. It gives us a chance to shift attention into the awareness of thought, rather than being captured in the thought. There's the Loving Blessing Practice, where we bring someone into our awareness whom we can feel absolute love for—and we beam them love. That's another way to directly experience the subtlety of our being. This loving presence isn't a physical thing, and yet it's an absolute energy that can be transmitted and shared.

There's the Living Practice, where we honor our feelings. When we're having a feeling, we bring attention to it, we honor it, we allow it to be directly experienced. It's an expression of the *Shakti*. We honor it—and we also honor that the feeling isn't all that we are. It's real. It's occurring. But it isn't all that we are. Because we're also the awareness of the feeling. So we let the feeling be directly experienced. When we become available to feelings in this way, they uncontract—they release on their own. If we allow them to be fully experienced, and we remember that we are also the awareness of the feeling, we can roam back out into that awareness—and realize that this awareness isn't limited to the body.

Notice right now, as you're reading these words, the part of you that's aware of these words is also aware of your breath. There's breath happening in your body—an in-breath, temporary. An out-breath, temporary. Each one, temporary. But notice how the awareness of those breaths isn't temporary. That awareness isn't a physical thing. And because it's not a physical thing, this is the part of you that can't die. It can't even age. It's the same awareness you've always been. It's not limited to your body. If it were, you'd only be aware of your body—but you're aware beyond the body. You're aware that the body is occurring in whatever environment you're in.

If you're in a room, you're aware the body's in a room. If you're outside, you're aware the body's in nature. On a walk. In a city. In a car, on an airplane, in a boat, a helicopter, a hang glider—wherever you might be. The awareness that you are is not limited to the body. You're aware that the body is in a location—and you're aware that location is on what we call a planet Earth. You're aware that this planet is in a solar system with other planets orbiting around a sun. And that solar system is in a galaxy. And that galaxy is in an even larger universe.

Now, let your attention expand beyond the edges of the body. Notice that what you are is not limited to the body's locality. The body is a particular location within the *Shakti*—within the primordial cosmic source energy that permeates all reality. The body is a location, but you're not limited to it. What you really are isn't local. Yes, there is a local expression you're experiencing—called the human life. But your awareness is beyond that. Roam out beyond the edges of the body. See if you can find an edge to the awareness. If you think you've found one, ask: Is that really an edge? Or is there still awareness beyond it? Expand in all directions. Can you find an edge to this subtlety that you are—this consciousness, this presence? What you are is edgeless, without constraints or requirements. This that you are—can't die. Can't age. Not only are you this—everyone is this.

This is the realm in which we can abide and realize that this reality isn't a problem to be solved. It's actually an adventure. An exploration of the possibilities of *Shakti*—of the primordial source energy expressing itself in varying subtleties and densities. We don't have a problem here.

Now, our attention can collapse into the limited perspective of The Wanter, and when it does, we will experience this reality again as a problem to be solved. That's where the suffering comes from. That's where the dilemma, the angst, the worry, and the fear come from—when we collapse into that limited perspective. However, when we let our attention expand into the larger perspective, we realize: this is all an adventure. We're getting to experience a human expression—a bio-organic sensory vehicle—that allows us to feel sensations, emotions, and experiences. All temporary. All real. We're not denying the *Shakti*. The *Shakti* permeates all form experiences. The *Shakti* is never separate. There really is one absolute energy that permeates all reality. The *Shakti* River—flowing everywhere, all at once, without the limits of linearity, logic, worry, or fear. None of this is actually a dilemma.

Now, we can experience that. This realm gives us the opportunity to explore that. What does worry feel like? What does anxiety feel like? What does depression feel like? We've all been conducting pretty extensive studies in these areas in our human lives. And yes, we will likely get pulled back into those perspectives again. That's the nature of this play of perspectives.

Remember, wherever we put our attention, that is what lights up. That is the perspective we embody. When attention gets pulled into the limited perspective of The Wanter, this reality looks like a problem. We try to control it. We try to get things to be safe and secure. We gather strategies along the way, trial-and-error attempts to make life feel manageable.

But no matter how many things we get to go our way, it doesn't bring lasting contentment. That's not the nature of The Wanter. It always needs more—more control, more safety, more attention, more love, more likes on social media. No matter how many likes The Wanter gets, it will always want another. That's its nature. It's insatiable. Never arriving in true happiness or contentment. When The Wanter gets what it wants, it may call itself happy. But that's not real happiness. That's just a temporary cessation in the wanting. A momentary silence. That's all.

So reflect: how many times did you want something, achieve it, and realize it didn't bring lasting fulfillment? That's not a failure—it's just not the nature of The Wanter. And yet— it is absolutely possible to shift our attention into the presence that we are. Into the awareness. Into the eternity that we are. Beyond the physical experience. Beyond The Wanter. I refer to it as our True Nature. Our eternal, absolute essence. Always here. Always accessible, simply by shifting attention. In this play of perspectives, we can shift at any moment. We can become aware that we're always in The Shakti River, wherever we go.

In the following chapters, we will explore practices that gently guide this shift of attention from The Wanter to True Nature, so you can directly experience the *Shakti* that you are.

ONE ORANGE TREE

LET'S IMAGINE FOR A MOMENT THAT WE LIVE ON A PLANET THAT has only one orange tree. For some strange reason, there's only one orange tree on the whole planet. A planet like Earth—similar population, similar size—and this orange tree can grow oranges, but for some strange and wonderfully mysterious reason that no one knows, it can't grow more orange trees, even though it can grow oranges.

On this very unusual planet, the percentage of people that will have ever tasted an orange would be very low because there's only one orange tree.

Let's say on that planet, I was one of the very few people that had ever tasted an orange, and you heard about that.

You said to me, "Mitch, I've heard that you've tasted the orange. Are they real? Do they exist? What do they taste like?"

You would have questions about this, naturally.

If the way that I respond to your beautiful questions is to describe an orange to you, I could try my best and speak about it being round. I could say it has this wrinkled orange skin that you peel, and it squirts juices as you peel it, revealing a segmented fruit inside. You peel those segments apart, bite into it, and it's simultaneously sweet and tart and juicy. I could try my best to describe an orange to you, and what you would receive from that is your mind would create a concept of what an orange tastes like based on my description.

Then, if someone asked you what an orange tastes like, you would say, "Yes, I know all about it. Let me tell you."

Your mind would be very willing to share the concept that was created based on my description within your mind. Then the person that you share that description with—*their* mind would create a concept of what an orange tastes like based on your description. Then if someone asked them, "Hey, do you know what an orange tastes like?" they would say, "Yeah, I'm an expert in oranges. I can tell you all about it. In fact, I'm going to have a workshop about this."

But all they would be able to share—no fault of their own—is their *concept* of an orange that their mind created based on the description they heard of what an orange tastes like. Down through the ages, these concepts would be shared on planet Earth.

That's what happened regarding the Truth about Source, and what reality is. There were organized groups of people down through the thousands of years that said, "We know what the truth is. Just believe what we say. Don't question it. Just have faith."

We notice that can only go so far, and it can actually create quite a lot of misunderstanding if all we're sharing is a concept about the nature of reality and just being told to believe it.

Another way, if we go back to our planet with the one orange tree, would be for me, instead of describing an orange to you, to hand you an orange and let you experience it for yourself. Then you would be able to peel the orange and experience the juiciness of it, the segmented fruit inside, the sweetness and the tartness. You would say to me, "Mitch, it's so much more than what you said."

I would say, "I know. Aren't they amazing?"

Now you would know what an orange tastes like because you've experienced it for yourself. You wouldn't have to believe in it. Your mind wouldn't be creating a concept of it. You know what an orange tastes like—the juices are running down your chin. You know what it tastes like: the texture, the smell, the color, the feel of it in your hands. The Truth of what an orange tastes like is revealed in the direct experience.

In the same way, the ancient lineages invite us into practices regarding the true nature of reality. I've had the great honor of being a part of many ancient lineages for years and years, and learned many different types of practices, and experienced them for years and years. I invite you into these practices so that you too can directly experience them.

Now, these old-school ancient practices build a momentum. They take time. We need to be in them *regularly* enough to experience the power that they inherently bring to us. If we are in them regularly enough, we'll start to experience the nuances and the subtleties.

Of the many, many practices I learned, I've shared several over the years, and there are a few practices that came to me when I began exploring with people.

The Name That Thought Practice is an example. That practice is a wonderful way that allows us to have a different relationship with our mind. It's a way of honoring our mind without having to be captured in the limited thoughts and beliefs that emerge from it.

The Problem Solver Mind Practice is for if we start to get pulled into a thought—a worry thought, let's say—the Problem Solver Mind Practice gives us a way to honor that, catch it early, and maybe not get pulled into that worry that could lead to anxiety and fear. There's a wonderful way in the Problem Solver Mind Practice, which I found organically, that allows us to rest back into the awareness and not be so captured in the mind.

The First Growl Practice is a wonderful way that organically came to me one day as a way to maybe catch the disturbances that start to rise up in us early, rather than getting pulled into them right at the beginning of the disturbance, which is why I call it the first growl.

If we can catch it early, right at the first growl, and simply ask, "What is my Wanter wanting that it's not getting?", what we start to notice is every disturbance we have—every time we're frustrated, annoyed, angry, sad, lonely, resentful—all of the various emotional disturbances we experience are coming from our Wanter wanting something that it's not getting. Our Wanter wanting something to be different than it is.

So if we can catch it right at the beginning of the distur-bance—the first growl—and ask, "What is my Wanter wanting that it's not getting?" that gives us a chance to rest back into the awareness of our Wanter. "Thank you so much, Wanter." The Wanter is just always trying to make things better for us. Then we can rest back into the awareness. We can let the breath be long and slow to help relax our nervous system. The more we explore these disturbances real early like this, the more we can change the habit of automatically getting pulled into them.

Now, sometimes the disturbance happens so quickly we're just affected. We're just in. And this is normal. It's okay to have feelings. It's so important to normalize this. We will have feel-ings. We will feel frustrated, annoyed, angry, resentful, hold grudges, feel sad, depressed, disappointed, dissatisfied. All of those things are normal, and they're all happening when our Wanter is wanting something that it's not getting.

When we get pulled in so fast and there's no time for those previous practices I mentioned, we have the Living Practice—an amalgamation of many of the things I learned on my journey—as a way to honor our feelings. We're going to have feelings; it's part of our human experience. We can honor our feelings, letting them be directly experienced without avoiding, stuffing them down, numbing out, or trying to solve or figure them out. We just let ourselves directly experience them, and then we can include that we're also the awareness of that emotional disturbance happening in our body. We notice where it's happening in our body and allow it to be directly experienced without any strategies or agendas.

We include that we're the awareness of the feeling. The feeling will eventually move its way through, and we evermore develop the capacity to honor our feelings without being wrecked by them, identified with and lost in them, or captured by them. This is the power of the Living Practice.

The Loving Blessing Practice is a powerful practice to liberate the love that we are—to let the direct experience of the love that we are be shared with others. It liberates the love. It allows us to directly experience the love that our Wanter has been seeking from someone outside of us, something external. We can directly experience that we are the love we've been looking for.

Another way to experience this love is through chanting. All the ancient lineages have chanting. Chanting is a circle, a vibrational circle of wholeness. When you enter into a rhythmic, repetitive circular chant, it's a vibration that tunes your body and allows the mind to relax out of linear, straight-line, logical thinking. You enter into the circle of the chant—round and round and round—and you start to experience the inherent wholeness of reality. It's a way of relaxing into non-linearity, the inherent oneness of reality.

All of these practices carry the potential to let us have a direct experience of this that we are, that is at ease. This pure awareness that we are—this stillness amidst all of the activity and the chaos of life. There is a stillness within us, an ease that's inherent, pure resting awareness. There's a natural joy within us. There's wonder and creativity and playfulness and lots of giggles in our True Nature.

This is the lovely possibility of the practices: they can let us have a direct experience of this eternal, true essence that we are. And the more that we let ourselves be in the practices regularly enough to start to receive the inherent benefit of them, the more likely we can enjoy the ride of this buck wild adventure that we call human life.

THE PRACTICES

NAME THAT THOUGHT ORIGINS

ONE YEAR AT THE ASHRAM, WE WERE INVITED INTO A PRACTICE called the Cat Mouse Meditation. We were invited to close our eyes and imagine that we are a cat sitting on the floor in a kitchen, and we're looking at the wall. Where the wall meets the floor, there's a little mousehole. We were invited to imagine that we are the cat—very relaxed, and also very attentively being available to see if a mouse comes out of the mousehole.

If a mouse came out of the mousehole, we were invited to consider that we could either chase after that mouse, or just notice what kind of mouse it was, and then rest back and see if another one came. What I realized from this Cat Mouse Meditation is that it was a metaphor they were inviting us into. It wasn't spelled out, but it was implicit to me that the cat was representing our attention, and the mouse was representing thought. If a mouse comes out of the hole, we notice what kind of mouse it is, and then we rest back and see if another one comes.

Many years later, after having learned that meditation, when I first started exploring with people in these ways that I now explore with people, the very first person I ever sat with was talking about how she had a lot of thoughts. Her mind was very busy, and she had trouble with meditation, because she had heard that in meditation you were supposed to try to quiet your mind. She noticed she could never do that, so she felt like a failure.

I shared with her that day, "Well, I have a different view on all of this than that. I don't ever approach meditation from the perspective that we're trying to quiet the mind—because the mind is going to have thought. That's part of what the mind does." I asked her, "Would you like to try something that I have found very useful?"

She said, "Sure."

So I said to her, rather than teaching her the traditional, classic Cat Mouse Meditation—in that moment—I imagined that she *was* the cat, and I invited her into the metaphor.

I said, "Be on the lookout for your next thought. Just be available. If your mind happens to send up a thought, and if the thought arrives, tell me what kind of thought it is."

Right away, she said, "I wonder if it's going to snow."

Then I said to her, "Okay, let's name that thought: 'I wonder if it's going to snow thought'. We've named that one. Okay, now let's, rather than going into that thought with our attention, properly honor it and name it, and now let's rest back and see if another one comes."

She paused for a moment and said, "If it snows, I need to get my car checked."

I said, "Okay, let's not let that story go too much further than that. Let's catch it early. 'Car checked if it snows thought'. Now let's rest back and see if another one comes."

She rested back and said, "How come I didn't already take my car in the other day?"

"Okay, let's catch that early: 'Why didn't I take my car in already thought.' Rest back, see if another one comes."

She rested back. There was a bit more of a gap where there was just quiet for a bit. She started giggling a little bit.

I asked, "What are you experiencing?"

She said, "Well, I'm not having any thoughts right now."

I said, "Fascinating. Notice how we're just being available. If a thought comes, we'll honor it. Name it. We're not trying to stop them, they're welcome to come. We're simply going to name them. If they come, honor them. Try to catch them early if we can. If we let them get too fully formed, we might get pulled into them. The intention is to catch it early as it's starting to rise up, name what kind of thought it is, honor it, and put the word 'thought' at the end of it."

"I'm having one about dinner," she said.

I said, "'What's for dinner thought'." And we rested back.

She said, "I should have gone to the grocery store."

I said, "Let's say, 'grocery store thought.'" Rest back.

It got quiet again. Her mind was quiet again. She started giggling, and then it was just quiet.

"Wow," she said.

I noticed that she was taking longer, slower breaths at this point. Her whole nervous system was more relaxed. Her body was relaxed. She commented that she was not having any thoughts, even without trying to quiet the mind. From this practice, she noticed that her mind was tending to be more quiet. We continued the practice, there was much more giggling and much less thought.

As the years have unfolded, I've shared this with many people; and in the early years, I used to refer to this practice as the *Joyful Noticer Practice*, because for me—and many that I had shared it with and invited into this practice—they would very often giggle or notice, and have a joyful response. Because very often, it was maybe the first time that they had ever experienced *not* having so much thought, and it was obvious to them that it was due to this practice, it was so much fun for them. It was like a delight that they weren't having thought.

So for years, I called it the *Joyful Noticer Practice.* Then one day, somebody that I had shared this practice with, she said, "Mitch, that *Name That Thought Practice* that you taught me is so powerful."

I said, "The what?"

She said, "You know, that *Name That Thought Practice* you taught me?"

"Which one is that?"

"The one where you have me sit and be on the lookout for the next thought, and if a thought comes, we name the thought and then we rest back and see if another one comes. You know, the *Name That Thought Practice.*"

I said, "That's a wonderful name for it."

"Well, that's what you called it," she said.

"Well, I don't remember calling it that. Do you mind if we call it that from now on?" I asked.

"Sure," she said.

So from that point on, I've always referred to it as the *Name That Thought Practice,* because, as she pointed out on that day, that is really the essence of the practice. We're honoring thought. We're not in any way trying to stop the mind. The mind will think—that's part of what minds do. The mind is simply just trying to help us. Our minds are very good at solving problems and analyzing, and organizing, and considering, and sifting through details, and being very helpful to us.

What we notice is that our mind will get going, and our attention will get pulled in, and it can create all kinds of stories and misunderstandings about who we are—worry, and regret, and all kinds of activity of the mind. This aspect of our mind that's very good at solving problems, if it doesn't have a particular problem to solve in this moment, it will very willingly go forward in time and try to solve something that *might* be a problem. It'll go round and round with it, but it can't solve it because it's not occurring yet. And that's all worry is. Worry is the problem-solver aspect of our mind going forward in time and trying to solve something that it can't solve because it's not occurring yet. That is worry.

In the same way, our mind—the problem-solver mind—will also go back in time and try to solve things that have already occurred, that our mind identifies as problematic. It can't solve those either, because they already occurred. When the problem-solver mind goes back in time and tries to solve things going back in time—which it can't solve—it creates regret, guilt, shame, and resentments.

Imagine if we could be more capable of not letting our attention get pulled into those kinds of thoughts that go forward in time, or the ones that go back in time, or the thoughts that are self-deprecating thoughts, self-judgmental thoughts. There are many types of thoughts that can create all kinds of disturbance for us.

If we had a way of not getting pulled into those—not a way of stopping them, but a way of not following those thoughts that then create all these worrisome moments, or regret moments, or self-deprecating moments—if we had a way to be less likely to get pulled into those types of thoughts, we could reduce the amount of stress and worry and psychological suffering that we create for ourselves, when our attention gets pulled into those types of thoughts.

You can also do this practice right on the fly—when you're out on a walk, when you're driving your car. You don't have to have your eyes closed. You can do this with your eyes open or your eyes closed. You can do this when you're in the grocery store, or when you're interacting with someone else. This is a practice that can go anywhere—wherever you go. It's also a good practice to do on a regular basis where you carve out some space in your day. Even if you just do it for a few minutes, simply sit down and be on the lookout for your next thought. It's that simple. I try to get people to do it several times a day. What I advocate for is five times a day—especially early on in the process.

That is the lovely possibility because–the more we're doing it, even if we just do it for a few minutes–we start building a momentum. We start changing the habit of our attention. That's what this all comes down to. Everything that we experience in any moment—whatever the quality of our experience is —it's determined by where we're putting our attention. If we let our attention get pulled into a worry thought, then we experience life through the perspective of worry. If we let our attention get pulled into a self-deprecating thought, then we experience life through the perspective of self-deprecation. If we let our attention get pulled into a regret thought, then we experience life through the perspective of regret.

When we do the *Name That Thought Practice*, we simply be available for the next thought. If a thought happens to come, we try to catch it early. That's the key. We try to catch it early, before it gets too fully formed. If it gets really formed, before you know it, you're in that storyline, and you're going on that suffering train that it'll take you on—and another thought will come and another—and it just starts building and spinning. I call it getting pulled into the hamster wheel of "ick world." It can be pretty icky on that hamster wheel. So if we do the *Name That Thought Practice*, we can change the habit of our attention where we don't always get pulled into those kinds of thoughts.

We just be available in the *Name That Thought Practice*. If a thought comes, we name it. We try to catch it early—the category of thought—like 'dinner thought', or 'weather thought', or 'my wife thought', or 'my husband thought', or 'my parents thought'. Whatever category it is. Try to catch it early as it's just starting to rise up. Name it, honor it, call it what it is: a thought. *"What's for dinner" thought*. Then we rest back, and we see if another one comes. Each time we're doing that, we're changing the habit of our attention so that our attention doesn't automatically get pulled into those thoughts. Then we rest back, and we see if another one comes.

Now, as you continue this practice, what I invite people to do, is to become ever more interested in this awareness that you're resting back into. Notice the nature of the awareness that's on the lookout for the thought. Notice the nature of your awareness—it's inherently calm. There's no worry here. There's no dilemma here. There's no self-deprecation going on here. There's no resentment or regrets.

I invite people to start becoming ever more interested in that, and noticing what that's like. Notice the nature of that awareness. Notice how the awareness is not a physical thing. It's real—it exists—but it's not a physical thing. The awareness. You couldn't grab hold of your awareness and show it to someone because it's not made out of matter. It's a subtler dimension of being. I invite people to rest in that subtlety, that presence, and then consider—because it's not a physical thing —that this is the part of you that can't die. It can't even age. It's the same awareness that you've always been and that you will always be. It's not in any way troubled. It has no dilemma. It has no agenda. It's just observing, peacefully, whatever is occurring. We rest in that. I often invite people to expand out into that awareness and see: can you find an edge to the awareness? Notice—if you expand out in all directions, does this awareness that you are, have an edge like your body does, or does it not have edges? Expand out. Can you find an edge to the awareness?

I'll invite people to expand out, out, out, and see. Notice how there's this resting, peaceful presence that you are, that is not in any way constrained or limited, or conditioned. It's just simply abiding peacefully, aware of whatever's occurring. I invite people to let their breath be a little bit longer and slower, and notice how there is this stillness, this peacefulness that you are.

When you do the *Name That Thought* Practice, it gives you a chance to experience your True Nature—your spirit. When we speak of spirit, this is your spirit. The awareness is your spirit. This is the part of you that can't die, can't even age. You've always been this, and you will always be this. You can roam out into the vastness of this presence that you are and realize that when you rest here, there's no worry here. There's no fear here. There's no dilemma here. There's just this resting presence that you are, that you've always been, and that you will always be.

NAME THAT THOUGHT PRACTICE

AFTER READING THROUGH THIS PRACTICE, WE INVITE YOU TO experience it directly. Name That Thought Practice is available as a guided audio on the *Wanter Dynamics & The Love We Are Podcast,* accessible on all major streaming platforms, YouTube, and at TheLoveWeAre.com.

I invite you to notice your breath. Notice how there's breath happening in the body. There are in-breaths, and there are out-breaths. Notice how there is this awareness that you are, that can notice when there's an in-breath and when there's an out-breath. Allow your breath to be a little bit longer and slower.

Now notice how you can let the breath elongate and become a little bit longer and slower in a very natural way, without any strain. Each in-breath, nice and long and slow, and each out-breath, nice and long and slow, filling the body. Relax and be on the lookout for your next thought. See if a thought comes. If so, name what kind of thought it is, catching it before it gets too fully developed.

If it gets really developed, it might pull our attention in, and we might go on the ride of that thought—and wherever that might take us could cause all kinds of dilemmas or emotions. But another possibility is to simply name the thought as it starts to arise.

Let's say the thought comes up: *I wonder what the weather will be tomorrow*—thought. Put the word *thought* at the end of it. Then rest back and see if another one comes. If there's a bunch of thoughts coming, bundle it, if there's no way you can name each individual thought. Sometimes they're so quick, so we bundle it; like a whole river of thought. Then we rest back. See if another one comes. If there's still a bunch, we can bundle it again. *That's a whole bunch of thought. Okay, let me rest back and see what comes next.*

Eventually, it'll just start to be a single thought. Just name it, put the word *thought* at the end of it, and rest back. See if another one comes.

Sometimes when we do this practice, it will get quiet. There won't be thought. So we rest in the stillness. If there is thought, we honor it. We're not against thoughts. We're not trying to stop thought. If a thought comes, we just notice what type of thought it is: 'What was that very mean thing that they said to me thought.' We just put the word *thought* at the end, rather than going into that story. Then rest back and see if another one comes.

Each time we do this, we're changing the habit of our attention. Instead of getting pulled into those thoughts—which could pull us into all kinds of stories, tales of woe of some sort or another—we can honor the thought, name it, put the word *thought* at the end. All it is is a thought. Then choose to rest back and see if another one comes. Each time we do this, we're changing the habit of our attention, changing that tendency of attention from automatically getting pulled into the thoughts and get pulled into that hamster wheel.

We have choice. We can name the thought, put the word *thought* at the end, and rest back.

There's this awareness that you are, that remains simply available to the possibility of a thought. Notice the nature of this awareness that you are. It's just existing—inherently calm, peaceful. There's no agenda regarding thought here. There's no dilemma. It's prior to the activity of the mind. There's just this abiding presence that you are. Notice the nature of that. Be loyal to that for a bit here. Notice what that's like. Your breath can be a little longer and slower.

Little by little, you may start to notice that you're just more interested in the resting awareness than all those thoughts that you tend to get pulled into. Notice the nature of this awareness that you are. It's not a physical thing. You couldn't grab hold of this awareness and show it to someone, and yet, it's real. It exists ongoingly. It continues to exist, but it's not a physical thing. Because it's not a physical thing, this is what you are that can't die, can't even age. The same awareness that you've always been, and that you will always be.

Because this awareness that you are is not a physical thing, notice it doesn't end at the edge of your body. It's not contained or constrained in your body. Notice—this awareness that you are is beyond your body, aware of the body, reading this book.

You are aware that the body exists on a planet. That planet is orbiting around a sun with other planets in a vast, vast space we call a solar system. And that solar system, as vast as it is, is in an even larger space we call a galaxy—of which there are billions and billions—in an even larger space we call a universe.

This awareness that you are is vast, spacious, without edge or boundary or constraint. You've always been this, and you will always be this. Allow your attention to remain loyal to this. And if a thought comes, we name it, put the word *thought* at the end, and we rest back and enjoy this vast, spacious awareness that you've always been—and you will always be.

CUP IN THE OCEAN

THIS IS A STORY ABOUT A VILLAGE OF PEOPLE WHO LIVE BESIDE A beautiful river. This river has water that naturally flows and is perfectly pure. They can drink the water right from the river without needing to filter it in any way. It is the water they use for their soup, to water their crops, to bathe, and to drink. It supports their lives.

The elders of this village tell the story of a mystical place called the ocean. They say the ocean is the source of all life because it's the source of their beautiful river that sustains them. Without it, they wouldn't survive. The elders share how this mystical place called the ocean, sends its water up into the clouds, and then the clouds bring that water and shower it on the land, creating their river. In the wintertime, there is snow. That snow melts into the river. This is the source of their river, which is the source of their lives.

This mystical place called the ocean is revered and honored within the village. They speak of it as being very far away. There's a girl who's heard these stories growing up, all through her years. She's heard about this mystical place called the ocean.

One year, as they're telling the story of the source of all life—she makes a decision. She is going to go on a quest in the direction the elders have said the ocean lies. She is going to go on a journey, a quest to discover: is it true? Is the source of all life the ocean? Is it real, or is it just a story the elders tell?

She gathers up provisions and puts them all in a backpack. One night, she sets out on the journey in the direction the elders described. She doesn't tell anyone, and she's determined to find out for herself.

On this journey, she encounters many situations and circumstances that require her to come up with solutions. Her mind is very helpful to her on this journey, solving challenges like adverse weather—rain, wind, hail, and all kinds of things along the way. She has to make temporary shelters to protect herself from these storms. Her mind is very helpful to her in solving these situations and figuring out solutions.

One day, she runs out of the food she brought with her, so her mind has to come up with alternate food sources. Then her water runs out, and she has to find new sources of water along the way. There are wild animal noises, and all kinds of unforeseen things that happen on her journey. Her mind is very, very useful to her. It is her ally, helping her solve problems on her quest to find out: is it true? The mystical place called the ocean —the source of all life. Does it exist?

Day after day, week after week, she continues on her journey. One day, she notices the land beneath her feet is shifting. It's a different color. It's white, very loose, and gives way when she walks on it. There are rolling hills of this white-colored earth that shifts beneath her steps. She notices the trees in this land are very unusual. They have trunks like the trees she's used to, but instead of limbs and branches coming out along the trunk, she sees the trunks go up, up, up, up, up . . . then at the very top, there's a little poof. She is in wonder and amazement at these trees that don't have regular limbs and branches like the ones she's known.

After navigating many situations and circumstances for weeks and weeks, one day she reaches a very tall dune made of this white-colored earth that gives way when she walks on it. She climbs to the very top. As she crests the hill, she looks over the other side—and she sees it. There it is. The mystical place called the ocean.

Instantly, she knows that it's true. It is actually true. The stories the elders have told all these years are *true*. She goes running down the backside of the dune. She takes off her shoes and socks, rolls up her pants, and stands at the edge of the source of all life—this mystical place called the ocean.

It lovingly, rhythmically caresses her feet—this cool rhythm of flow. In and back out. She looks out as far as she can see, off into the horizon, and it goes on forever. It is vast and infinite—this source of all life, this mystical place called the ocean. It's true. It's true. It's true!

She is completely at peace. Her breath is long and slow, naturally. She's content, calm, and in bliss. She has found it. It's true. The source of all life continues to very lovingly, slowly caress her feet, coming in and going back out. It's true. It's true.

She is completely at peace. Her breath is long and slow. She's found it. It's true.

Then a thought comes into her mind: *How will I ever be able to explain and prove this to everybody back at the village?* Her breath shifts to upper-chest, shallow breathing. She's fretting. She's worried. She's stressed. She can't figure out how to solve this situation. *How can I prove that this mystical place called the ocean is real? How will I ever explain it?*

She grabs her drink cup from her backpack. She holds it in both hands, arms extended as far as she can toward the mystical place called the ocean. She's holding the cup, breathing heavily.

Someone who lives in this land has witnessed all of this. They walk up to her and say, "What is causing you such trouble? Why are you so stressed?"

She looks at the person as she continues to hold her drink cup out, full arms extended toward the ocean. She says, "No matter how hard I try, I can't get the ocean to fit in my cup."

The person who lives in this land takes a big in-breath and a big out-breath and says to her, "Yes, this is true. There's another way."

She says, "Please tell me. You say there's another way. Tell me—what is it? What is this other way you speak of?"

The person looks at her with such love and kindness and says, "You can throw your cup into the ocean."

In this beautiful story, the cup is symbolic of our mind. The ocean is symbolic of the infinite, absolute essence that permeates all reality—the source of all existence. At the moment when she was completely at peace—when she had discovered it was true—she was in bliss. She was calm. Then her mind came in to try to help. To try to solve: *How can we prove this back at the village? How can we explain this to everyone?* Her mind was trying to solve this for her. And it took away the peace. It took away the tranquility, the ease, the bliss. She was stressed. Her breath became upper-chest shallow breathing. Her mind was trying to come up with a solution. *Please, please, please.*

When she said to the person, "No matter how hard I try, I can't get the ocean to fit in my cup." That's true. We cannot fit the infinite into the finite. We can't fit the infinite, absolute truth of existence into the cup of the mind. When we have mystical experiences of the Truth, our mind will try to understand it, to make sense of it—but it won't be able to. All it will do is cause stress, concern, and worry.

So, the possibility, in any moment when we notice our mind is coming in and trying to solve something that's beyond its ability to know, we can throw our cup into the ocean. We can let go into the infinite—into the unknown.

The mind operates in the realm of logic and reason—the known. It doesn't in any way like when there is unknown. When it is unresolved, when it is in-flux. Our mind will always try to get everything solved, with the idea that *then* everything will be okay. There will be many moments on our spiritual awakening journey where the mind will come in and try to understand the infinite source of all existence—and it isn't capable of that. It doesn't work.

In those moments, the lovely possibility is that we can let go of the need to narrow it down into some box the mind can understand—and throw our cup into the ocean. Let go into the unknown, and enjoy the ride.

PROBLEM SOLVER MIND PRACTICE

LET'S EXPLORE THIS ASPECT OF OUR MIND THAT I CALL THE Problem Solver Mind. It's a very helpful part of us. It's excellent at solving problems that are happening right now. If we're making guacamole in the produce section, our Problem Solver Mind is great at figuring out which avocados are too green, which are too ripe, how many we want, whether we need onion or jalapeño, or what else we'd like to add. If we're driving home and the light turns yellow, it quickly helps us decide whether to stop or go. Just now, as I was sitting here with the windows open in my studio, a thunderstorm started rolling in. I stood up to close the windows so the rain wouldn't come in, and my Problem Solver Mind was right there to help. It's great at handling what's happening in this moment.

In the case of an actual emergency, there's also a very natural process that kicks in. If you were out on a walk and heard a strange sound, looked over and saw a mountain lion, your body would immediately start pumping adrenaline. That's the fight-or-flight response. The heart rate would elevate, more blood would get pumped to the muscles, all to give you a better chance of running away or staying to fight. It's a whole chemistry lab—adrenaline, cortisol, all the stress hormones—designed to help us survive. This same process happens for any real emergency. A hurricane, a tornado, a house fire, drowning —this system is beautifully built to kick in when needed.

But here's where it gets interesting. If there's not an actual problem *right now*, our Problem Solver Mind will often go forward in time to look for one. It imagines something that might go wrong—like if we're planning a hike and start worrying about the possibility of a mountain lion. The mind spins on it, and the body can't tell the difference. It starts pumping adrenaline, the heart races, cortisol flows, all because of worry. But there's no mountain lion here. We're just imagining it. That energy doesn't get burned off by running or fighting, so it stays in the body. That leftover chemistry is what we call anxiety. That's why anxiety feels physical—jittery, sweaty, like we might pass out. It's the result of the chemistry lab getting activated for something that isn't actually happening.

There's a simple sequence here. If there's no worry, there's no anxiety. We don't have worry if the Problem Solver Mind doesn't go forward in time trying to solve something that isn't here yet. In the same way, the Problem Solver Mind also likes to go back in time. It'll revisit something that already happened—some choice we made, something someone did or didn't do—and it will spin and spin: "If only this had happened . . ." "Why didn't they do that?" "I should have . . ."

It's trying to solve it. But it can't. It's already done. And because it can't change it, the mind spins, which triggers regret, shame, guilt, resentment, blame, heartbreak. That's not wrong. The Problem Solver Mind is simply trying to help. It's not the enemy. It just doesn't realize it can't solve things in the past or the future.

There's a beautiful possibility here. When we notice our Problem Solver Mind has gone forward into worry, or backward into regret or resentment, we can pause and ask a simple question: "Hey, Problem Solver Mind, is there anything of benefit that can be done right now regarding that?"

If the answer is yes, we might get an impulse to add it to a to-do list or make a phone call. Then, we do that thing.

But most of the time—almost always—the answer will be no. When it's no, we can gently say, "Thank you so much, Problem Solver Mind. Thank you for trying to help me with that. But we can't do anything about it right now."

Then we bring our attention back to the breath. Nice, long, slow breaths. In through the nose, letting the belly slowly expand, and out through the mouth, letting the belly gently press back in. Because the body knows that if we're breathing long and slow, there's no emergency. If there were a mountain lion here, we wouldn't be breathing like this. We'd be gasping, hyperventilating, running. When we breathe long and slow, the nervous system gets the message: oh, there's actually no emergency. The heart rate settles, the adrenaline stops pumping, the cortisol eases, the entire chemistry lab can return to a calm, natural state.

If we can catch it early—when the Problem Solver Mind first tries to run forward into worry or backward into regret—we can stop a lot of unnecessary suffering before it builds. But if we don't catch it early and we're already feeling regret, guilt, heartbreak, shame, resentment, then it's time for what I call the Living Practice. That's where we just let ourselves fully feel whatever energy is here, without pushing it away. We will explore the Living Practice in an upcoming chapter.

In any moment, we have this option. We notice if our Problem Solver Mind is trying to solve something forward in time, which creates worry and anxiety, or backward in time, which creates regret, shame, guilt, heartbreak, resentment, or blame. We ask it, "Hey Problem Solver Mind, is there anything of benefit that can be done right now?"

When the answer is no, we thank it, because it's only trying to help. "Thank you so much, Problem Solver Mind. Thank you for trying to help me with that. But we can't do anything about it right now."

Then we come back to the breath. Take a nice, long, slow in-breath through the nose, letting the belly expand, and long, slow out-breath through the mouth, belly pressing gently back in. Resting here. Letting the system calm. Returning to this simple presence, this ease that is always available.

We don't have to create all that unnecessary suffering for ourselves. We see we have a choice. Where we place our attention determines what we experience. Wherever we let our attention go, that's what lights up. Instead of letting it be pulled into old stories or future worries, we can return to this breath, to this moment, and rest in the natural peace of our True Nature.

FIRST GROWL PRACTICE

In all these years of exploring the nature of our experience, I've noticed that every disturbance we have comes from what I call The Wanter. The Wanter, which is very much our ally, is always trying to make things better for us. That's its function in every moment: to look out for us, to make sure we eat when we're hungry, get hydrated when we're thirsty, seek out the right temperature when we're cold or too hot. The Wanter is incredibly useful, very helpful. Yet every disturbance we have still comes from The Wanter—wanting something to be different than it is. That's what creates frustration, annoyance, anger, resentment, disappointment, sadness, or regret. Every disturbance arises because The Wanter is resisting what's actually occurring, wanting it to be something else.

This became especially clear to me one day when I was driving across town to an appointment. As I drove up the on-ramp and could finally see the highway ahead, there it was: bumper-to-bumper traffic. Instantly, I felt that growl inside. But there was enough awareness in me at that time to remember: every disturbance comes from The Wanter. So right in that moment—right at the beginning of the growl—I simply wondered: "What is my Wanter wanting that it's not getting right now?"

The moment I asked that question, I noticed I was now the awareness of my Wanter. I wasn't captured in it, wanting the traffic to disappear, feeling frustrated or upset. I was resting back in a deeper place of consciousness, aware of this aspect of human nature. It was so clear, "Of course my Wanter is wanting there not to be bumper-to-bumper traffic."

I felt so much gratitude for my Wanter in that moment: "Thank you so much, Wanter. All this life you've been looking out for me, trying to make things ideal, optimized, always on the lookout for how to make everything the best for me. Thank you for the thousands of moments you've actively tried to do that." And then I communicated, "I just want you to know, we don't actually have control over this."

Right then, I noticed I began breathing long and slow, the way I learned at the ashram. In through the nose, letting the belly expand; out through the mouth, letting the belly gently press back in. This style of breathing—pranayama—naturally relaxes the nervous system, slows the heart rate, calms the muscles. I realized this was a way to avoid getting pulled into the suffering I would have created if I'd stayed stuck in my Wanter, growling at the traffic. That would've led to more thoughts: "Why does this always happen to me? This is so unfair. Now I'm going to be late." It may even spiral into self-loathing: "I should've left earlier. I'm such an idiot."

All of that could have happened—and yet it didn't—because I caught it at the first growl. That day in traffic was the origin of what I now call the First Growl Practice. It became clear that every disturbance is simply The Wanter wanting something to be different than it is. I also noticed something interesting: when I was upset about the traffic, I wasn't upset there was traffic for everyone—I was just upset there was traffic for me. The Wanter is very narrowly focused. That's its design.

It doesn't care about anyone else; it only wants to optimize things for me. That's why we can be selfish, or why others sometimes seem selfish to us. They're just in their Wanter.

So this became the invitation: if we can catch the disturbance right at the beginning—at the first growl—and ask, "What is my Wanter wanting that it's not getting right now?" we immediately shift. Now we're the awareness of The Wanter. We're not trapped inside it. We can thank our Wanter, "Thank you so much for looking out for me," and then take a long, slow breath.

When we shift our attention to that long, slow breath, the body knows there's no emergency. When we're caught in the growl, the body pumps adrenaline, raises the heart rate, floods the muscles for action. But when we breathe long and slow, the whole system settles. From here, we can see options we wouldn't see if we were still captured. Maybe I text the person I'm meeting to let them know I'll be late. Maybe I get off at the next exit and try to find a back way. Maybe there are no good side streets, so I put on some music, or even send love to everyone else stuck in traffic. That's something our True Nature would do—our true self would absolutely send loving blessings to all these other people in the same situation. The Wanter wouldn't, but the awareness we are would.

This isn't about pretending The Wanter's wrong. Often The Wanter is seeing things quite accurately. There *is* bumper-to-bumper traffic. But if we look *only* through The Wanter's lens, it becomes a problem that creates suffering, which clouds our ability to navigate wisely. If we catch it at the first growl, thank The Wanter, breathe long and slow, we can then explore options from a place of spaciousness and clarity. "This traffic is what's occurring. What are my options here?" We try one. If that doesn't work, we accept that and look for the next. We keep showing up for the lovely possibility of finding a solution. If we're not attached to a particular outcome, when things don't go our way—which happens often—we can stay agile and explore the next option.

That's the heart of this practice. In every moment, situations will arise that don't go how our Wanter wants them to go. If we get pulled in, we create a disturbance. But if we catch it at the first growl—ask what The Wanter's wanting, thank it, breathe long and slow—we can rest back into our True Nature and meet life in a wise, loving, empowered way. We keep showing up, moment by moment, for the lovely possibility—without needing it to turn out any certain way.

TAPAS LOKA

LET'S TALK ABOUT OUR LIVED HUMAN EXPERIENCE. THERE'S SUCH a wide variety of experiences we can have from day to day—and sometimes it's quite challenging. Things happen that we'd rather not have happen. This place can be intense. It's important to honor that. When those unwanted experiences occur, they can pull us in. We might get captured in a prolonged flow of suffering. That's very real. Very likely.

Something I learned at the ashram is that, in the ancient lineages, they refer to this human realm—this earth experience —as a *tapas loka*. *Loka* is a Sanskrit word for realm or place. *Tapas* literally means heat. But more fully, it points to *transformational heat*. This earth is a realm of transformational heat. When things happen that we don't want, there's friction—suffering. If we resist it, it creates more heat. But if we're willing to turn toward it, to let ourselves directly experience it, that heat becomes transformational. That's the invitation of *tapas loka*.

The Living Practice I invite people into is a way of honoring the *tapas* of this *loka*. It means turning toward the disturbance.

Facing it, instead of moving away. Letting our lived experience be a path of ever-deepening into our true essence.

When I first learned about this at the ashram, as the Swami spoke about tapas, all my attention drew inward. My eyes closed, and I dropped into a vivid inner realm. I found myself lying on my stomach on cracked, dry red clay earth. I was dying of dehydration—my body turning to solid matter. The pain was intense. I lifted my head and realized I'd been lying next to a river all along. With my last bit of strength, I raised my arm to scoop up some water. Suddenly, there was a pan in my hand, and I dipped it into the river. As I brought it to my mouth, I saw the water was filled with impurities. It would only make me sicker. In that moment, I understood: this water had been pure at its source, deep in the earth, but as it traveled—day after day, year after year—it picked up impurities.

Just like us. As we live these human lives, we pick up beliefs like, "I'm not good enough," or "I'm unworthy." We contract these impurities around painful experiences. These impressions are like the impurities in the water.

Then the vision shifted. I was standing at a stove, turning the burner to high flame. I placed the pan of water on it. The heat would allow the impurities to be boiled off. As the water heated, suddenly I could see all the individual H_2O molecules. They were yelling at me—angry, suffering, blaming me: "Why would you do this? Turn it off! We don't deserve this!"

But I could see from a different perspective. I knew this was the most loving thing I could do: to let them go all the way through the heat. Eventually, the impurities boiled off. I turned off the flame. The little H_2O molecules stood there, hands together at their hearts in *namaste mudra* (palms pressed together at the heart), thanking me: "Thank you for not turning off the heat. Now we've returned to our natural state. Now we can be inherently beneficial."

I opened my eyes, looked around at all of us sitting with the

Swami at the ashram, and realized: *We are the water molecules. This earth is the pan. There will be heat.*

Our Wanter, of course, always wants to avoid discomfort. That's its job—if we're cold, it moves us to warmth. If we're hungry, it seeks food. And when emotional heat comes—sadness, loneliness, frustration, anger—our Wanter wants to move away. But if we're willing to go right into that heat—to directly experience the sensation in the body without trying to solve it, fix it, or make it go away—something remarkable happens.

Over time, the heat uncontracts those energies. The sadness, the anger, the loneliness—they start to release. It takes however long it takes. But as they uncontract, we discover something profound: they were always source energy, just temporarily condensed. When the contraction dissolves, we open into the simplicity of eternity.

Tapas is a portal into wholeness. By being willing to move toward the heat—from the inside—we discover that every contraction was simply the infinite source of all existence, expressing itself in a temporary form.

LIVING PRACTICE ORIGINS

Regarding the origins of the Living Practice, one of the core practices I share with people I explore with, really began with what I learned at the ashram about *tapas* (transformational heat) and what I learned from my mom about facing strong emotions instead of moving away from them. We can let ourselves honor our feelings, rather than distracting from them, trying to figure them out, solve them, numb them with substances, or avoid them. We can turn toward them, and be willing to burn in them.

Our Wanter will have no interest in this. The Wanter always wants to move away from discomfort—distract, avoid, or reach for some fleeting comfort that won't bring real relief, because the energy remains stored inside.

The true roots of this became clear to me at the ashram but also started with what my mom showed me, through how she met me in my feelings. When I had strong emotions, she invited me to let them be felt and honored them. Sometimes she made it very clear that it was the *only* way.

When I was seven years old, coming home from elementary school, and as I approached the house I felt a dread in my stomach. I never knew what I'd walk into. At this point, my mom had started dating a man. Before that, it had always just been my mom, my little sister, and me—ever since my dad left when I was a baby. This man was very temperamental and could get mean when he drank. My mom never drank, so this was new and confusing. I could see how hard it was on her, on my sister, and on me. I didn't understand why he was even there. Of course, now I can see—she was a single mom, just nineteen when she had me, living in a small town with few options.

That day I walked in and saw my mom had been crying. She was wearing a scarf around her forehead in a way she normally didn't. I climbed into her lap and gently moved the scarf aside. There was an indentation in her forehead—the exact shape of the pinky ring that man wore on his right hand. As soon as I saw it, I went into a primal rage. I jumped off her lap and ran into my room. I could hear her chasing me. I grabbed my baseball bat—intent on finding him and hurting him for what he did. But she was faster. She caught me, took the bat out of my hand, and sat down holding me tight. She wouldn't let me act on my rage. She held me there and said, "Mitch, if you do this, you'll be doing exactly what he just did to me."

I kept pushing, trying to get away, fists clenched, jaw tight, determined to go get him. But no matter how hard I tried, she held me. I just had to face it and burn in it—and I did *not* want to. My Wanter wanted to make sure he never hurt her again.

As she held me, she said, "Mitch, from the moment you came into my life, I've experienced your gentleness, your playfulness, your kindness, your sweetness, and your tenderness. I know this is hard for you and you want to help me, but I love you too much to let you do something that would pull you away from your pure heart."

That moment was so intense. I could feel her strength. She

was helping me—teaching me to face feelings rather than act on them. To burn in the intensity without distracting, fixing, or numbing. And little by little, the feeling eased. I could feel how much she loved me. It faded and eventually released. I hugged her and thanked her. When I reflect on the origins of the Living Practice, it all began there—with her. She taught me how to face emotions instead of avoiding them.

The first person I ever sat with was someone who called me one day while I was preparing for a painting's arrival—a painting I call *Heart of Being*. The phone rang. I answered.

She said, "Mitch, I had a vision just now during meditation. In it, I was sitting with you. You were teaching me spiritual practices, telling me stories, and we were chanting together. Would that be a possibility?"

I said, "Yes. Come on over."

During our time together, she began feeling very strong emotions. I invited her to share everything—what happened, what she was feeling—so the energy could be honored and heard. Then I invited her to turn toward where she felt it in her body. It was in her gut. Slowly, I offered her this way that had become so natural to me, something I called *burning in it*. That's what I'd say to myself, *I need to burn in this.*

I invited her to do the same.

As she let herself fully feel it, I said, "Now that you're feeling this—without trying to fix, solve, or change it—you're showing yourself that you can feel your feelings. You don't have to move away, numb out, or distract yourself."

Little by little, the feeling started to uncontract and release. When she opened her eyes, she was filled with wonder. She asked, "What is the name of this practice?"

And it just tumbled out of me: "The Living Practice." As if it had already named itself. Since that day, it's continued to reveal why it chose that name. It works best when it becomes a part of our life—*a living practice*. Something alive. Something present in our everyday experience.

It's a way of showing ourselves we don't have to avoid strong emotions. We can let them be directly experienced, in this beautiful, natural way that called itself The Living Practice.

We can feel our feelings. Honor them. Allow them to be experienced—not be captured by them, overwhelmed by them, or lost in them. Because once we're truly feeling them in the body, we also become aware of the awareness. It sounds funny, but we become aware of the awareness of the feeling—and see that the feeling isn't all we are. It doesn't define us in totality.

As the feelings and emotions uncontract, however long it takes, we rest back into that awareness. It releases itself. We can't have an agenda for how long it takes. But when it does, there's such liberation. Because we've demonstrated to ourselves that we can feel our feelings. And those feelings? They're actually a portal—into the deeper realization that we are an eternal presence, utterly untouched by the flow of human emotion.

So we can let ourselves be available to this process. And let it be a Living Practice.

LIVING PRACTICE

AFTER READING THROUGH THIS PRACTICE, WE INVITE YOU TO experience it directly. The Living Practice is available as a guided audio on the *Wanter Dynamics & The Love We Are Podcast,* accessible on all major streaming platforms, YouTube, and at TheLoveWeAre.com.

Welcome to this moment, exactly as it is. Allow yourself to directly experience whatever you're feeling in your body right now, without any resistance. There's no agenda here, no strategy, nothing to analyze or figure out. Simply be willing, in a raw and real way, to be completely available to this direct experience, letting it be exactly as it is, and allowing it to flow, much like water in a river. Your experience is a river of energy, naturally moving. Notice how whatever arises does not define all that you are, because there is also that in you which is aware— like a presence sitting on the bank of this river, watching it flow by. This awareness is completely accepting and receptive, without any need to control or move away. Let yourself relax into this moment as it is.

As you notice the sensations present in your body, remember that they don't define all of you. We honor this physical experience, as well as the emotional and mental experiences, and we also honor the nonphysical aspect of you—this pure awareness that observes it all. This awareness has never been altered or harmed by anything that's ever happened. No life event has ever touched this eternal presence that you've always been and always will be. As sensations flow, let them flow. If emotions arise, let them flow. If thoughts come, let them flow too. All of it is welcome here, without any agenda. Completely open, accepting, and receptive. There is this awareness that you are, resting, unaltered and unharmed—always.

Allow your breath to be long and slow. Each in-breath, a little longer and slower, each out-breath, a little longer and slower. Notice how each breath is temporary—it has a beginning, a duration, and a completion. But this awareness that you are is continuous. Through all the days, weeks, months, and years of your life, you've been this same awareness. Because it's not a physical thing, it cannot age or die. This awareness existed before this body, through many lifetimes—different bodies, different sizes, skin colors, genders, languages, circumstances—and yet nothing ever altered this eternal presence that you are.

Check in again with the body and notice whatever is there, knowing it will shift and change. That's the nature of the physical realm—everything has a beginning, a duration and a completion. All of it is an expression of this wholeness that not only you are, but everyone is. Not everyone realizes this, but everyone is this. We can honor the physical, the emotional, the mental, and also this deeper truth: we are, all of us, this timeless, eternal presence. You may encounter other beings acting from their own Wanter, sending behaviors your way that come from their own wants and resistances. You can understand this, accept it, and not take it personally. Each experience is a temporary occurrence: beginning, duration, completion.

Now let your awareness expand beyond the edges of your body. Notice: does this awareness have an edge? Let it expand. You're aware of the body in a room, the room in a building, the building on a planet, the planet among other planets orbiting a sun in vast space.

This solar system in a galaxy, this galaxy among billions of galaxies in an even larger universe. Notice how this awareness you are has no edge, no boundary, no constraint. You've always been this vast, spacious, pure presence—absolute consciousness, everywhere at once. Rest in that.

Let your breath continue long and slow. The body may have waves of energy—sensations, emotions, thoughts—rising and falling, like waves on an ocean. We can experience these waves as separate, or we can see them as expressions of the ocean of consciousness itself. No experience in any lifetime has ever altered this calm, peaceful presence that you are. Notice how inherently peaceful this awareness is. It requires no effort to be this. It is naturally calm, patient, compassionate, and infinitely wise. From here, we would never harm another being. We would naturally respond with understanding and love.

Everything that occurs is temporary: it has a beginning, a duration, and a completion. We can allow it all, rest in this presence, and navigate life from true acceptance and deep wisdom. This presence you are is what makes you most capable of choosing, exploring, and responding wisely. And not only are *you* this—*everyone* is this. No one is ever truly harmed at this deepest level. The body, emotions, and mind are all affectable—temporary waves of emotions and experiences. But what you truly are cannot be affected by anything in this physical dimension. So we honor whatever arises, navigate with acceptance, and rest in this presence you've always been and always will be.

Let your breath be long and slow. Let the body relax deeply. Notice the feet and allow them to soften and release. The ankles, shins, calves, knees, thighs, pelvis—softening and letting go. The lower belly and lower back, mid-belly, mid-back, upper back and chest—relaxing and releasing. Let the shoulders drop, arms soften, elbows, forearms, wrists, and hands completely release. The neck and throat, the jaw, mouth, cheeks, nose—softening and letting go. The eyes, forehead, ears, back of the head, top of the head—all at ease. The whole body, completely relaxed.

Now rest in this spacious awareness, knowing this presence is what you are, what you've always been, and what you will always be. It is vast, eternal, peaceful, and wise. Spacious, beyond all edges or limits. Rest here, in this inherent truth. You are this—always have been, always will be.

LIBERATING THIS LOVE WE ARE

MANY YEARS AGO AT THE ASHRAM, I WAS INVITED INTO A practice they said was very powerful—something handed down through generations. It had a Sanskrit name: *Ashirwad*, which in English can be translated as *loving blessing.*

In this practice, we were invited to bring someone into our awareness—anyone we could feel unconditional love toward. It could be a person, an animal, any being. We would let the love that we are be shared, emanated, beamed toward them. We didn't even need to know where they physically were; we simply held them in our awareness and sent that love.

Inevitably, what tends to happen in this practice is that someone our Wanter is holding a grudge against will show up. We were taught that if this happens, we can see whether the love that we are can flow toward them. That's the choice point. When someone we have a grievance or disturbance with appears, we can either hold onto our story—our grievance list that justifies withholding love—or we can let it go. That is the choice. If you can't let it go, that's okay. No judgment. You simply return to the original being—the one you can easily love—and begin again.

My teacher would say, "Eventually, this builds a momentum. There can be a liberation of the love that we are through this very powerful, transformational practice that's been handed down for generations."

When I started consistently doing this practice, it was deeply liberating to feel that unconditional love—the love we are. The practice resonated so strongly with me. I stayed with it every day. What I began to notice was that each time I did the Loving Blessing Practice, a certain image would appear. Two young Mormon men, in black pants, white shirts, ties, with satchels of literature slung over their shoulders—coming to convert me.

As soon as they appeared in my awareness, I noticed that the love I am would collapse. I wasn't willing to send them love. My Wanter had all kinds of reasons to justify it. I'd had many uncomfortable experiences growing up with people trying to convert me. I felt pressured. I built a strong belief that you should never try to convert others. I stood firmly on that soapbox, determined to point out the flaw in it. I was fervent—adamant. That stance formed in my youth from all those experiences.

There were even kids at school—because they were Mormon—who acted like they were better than me, who said hurtful things, demeaned me for not being Mormon. I had a whole grievance list tied to that history.

So every time I did the Loving Blessing Practice, and those two Mormons walked toward me in my mind, I shut down. The love I am was withheld. And I felt completely justified. Day after day, I practiced. Day after day, the same image would arise. The field would collapse.

But we were invited to remember: at that moment, it's a choice. Hold onto the grievance—or let it go. If you can't, that's okay. Just return to someone you *can* send love to.

My teacher would say, "It'll build momentum. Don't judge yourself. Just begin again."

So I kept practicing. Day after day, week after week, month after month. And still, every time, the image of the two Mormons came. I even reached a point where I put my hands together at my heart and said, "Dear Divine Grace, could I please have one Loving Blessing Practice without Mormons trying to convert me?"

But they kept coming. And just as my teacher promised, over time, the momentum began to build.

One day during the practice, they appeared again: black pants, white shirts, ties, satchels. I noticed my hands clenched into fists, my jaw tightened, a growl even emerged: *here they are again!*

The love field collapsed. My body was in full reaction. I realized—I was so right. So *righteous*. I was aware of how righteous I felt. Suddenly, I saw it: I was doing the very thing I accused them of doing to me. I was being righteous. I believed I was right and they were wrong. That was always my story of those interactions.

But here I was, clenched in that same rightness. Then I realized: I get to be right, but I don't get to be love. I get to be right, but I don't get to be free. I'm here, in this prison of rightness.

Yes, I could hold onto my grievance. I was "right" about what they did. But I couldn't be love while still holding it. In that split second, something broke open. I had no more interest in being right. I was more interested in being love. In that instant, I felt the liberation of the love we are. Tears of gratitude streamed down my face. I shared the love that I am with them —so fully, so naturally. It was pure freedom.

As my journey continued—day after day, week after week— other people I held grudges against appeared in my practice. One by one, those grudges dissolved. Just as my teacher said, the momentum grew. I became more interested in being love than being right.

Two years later, the final person appeared: my father, who left us when I was a baby. My mom was pregnant with my sister at the time, and I was just a little guy. I have no conscious memories of him. Just a lifetime of not having a father—talk about a grievance list. Every time he came into my awareness, the love I am would collapse. My Wanter had plenty of reasons to withhold love. Until one day, just like with the others, it finally released. I realized again: I can hold onto this and be right, but I don't get to be love. I can be right, but I don't get to be free.

Then there was no one left—no person, no thing—being withheld from the liberation of the love we are.

Eight or nine years later, I was out walking in my neighborhood. I turned a corner, and there they were: two Mormons, black pants, white shirts, ties, satchels. I was so relieved—because I didn't feel any urge to turn and run. I didn't feel the old drive to counter them, or prove a point, or defend anything. None of that. There was just love. I was so grateful for all the years of the Loving Blessing Practice—because without it, I'd still be holding onto my rightness. I never would've had this moment.

I felt such compassion. I thought of all the doors slammed in their faces, all the things people said—or things I myself had once said. As we approached each other, they looked at me and seemed relieved by the look on my face.

They said, "Sir, can we walk with you today?"

"Absolutely," I said. "I'm out on an exercise walk—want to match my pace?"

"Absolutely," they said. So now the three of us walked together, side by side. The one nearest to me introduced himself. "My name is Brother so-and-so of the Church of Latter-day Saints, and this is my partner Brother so-and-so of the Church of Latter-day Saints, and we believe . . ." And he shared a Mormon belief. Then another. Then another. Eight or nine in total. The whole time, I was just relieved I didn't need to counter him or argue or fix anything. None of that was there. Just love.

Then he paused and said, very firmly, "So, what do *you* believe?"

It was like time stopped. In a split second, I had a vision: these two young men, as little boys—four or five years old—sitting in a Mormon church with family all around. At the front was someone very important, saying all the beliefs they'd just shared with me. Every Sunday. Over and over. From the pulpit, from their parents, from everyone.

I saw how belief systems form. The human mind is so malleable, so eager for a system to make sense of this wild life. It grabs hold of beliefs, wraps itself in them for security. It loves being right—on the "right team," with all the answers. There's comfort in that.

Then I saw myself at four or five. I didn't grow up in religion, but I was indoctrinated another way. Told I was Mitchell Rosacker, from Colorado, an American, athletic, smart. I saw that's how the "religion of Mitch" happened. It's the same. Just another system. But, what we truly are is prior to all of that. We are these eternal, divine beings who then take on identities, beliefs, systems. All of that came in a flash. Then I was back to real time. The question completed itself: "So what do *you* believe?"

And what tumbled out of me was, "Well, actually, less and less."

It just came out. Because what we are is prior to all the beliefs. When I said that, it was like a transmission of truth. They went quiet. For about twenty minutes, we walked together, three embodiments of love, silent, smiling.

Then the young man nearest to me looked over and asked, "Who are you?"

Again, I didn't plan it. It just tumbled out: "I am what you are. We are this love."

Quiet again. Twenty more minutes. Just pure presence.

Then he asked from such a sweet, pure place, "How did you get this way?"

What spilled out was, "I just kept turning my attention within and directly experiencing this love we are, which is prior to all the beliefs."

It was quiet again. Another twenty minutes of walking, just being. Finally, we reached my house. I said, "I want to thank you both so much for this wonderful walk. I'm so grateful for what we shared."

The young man said, "Can I come talk with you another day?"

"Sure," I said. "You know where I live."

"Me too?" his friend added.

"Absolutely."

Then he asked, "Can I give you a hug?"

"Of course." He came in and started to cry, holding on tight. Tears of gratitude. Then his friend asked for a hug too. Same thing—crying, holding on. It was so sweet.

Then the first young man looked at his satchel, then at me, then at the satchel again. I could see his Wanter stirring. He asked, "Can I give you some of our literature?"

I laughed. "You could, but as soon as I go inside, it's going straight in the trash."

He laughed too. "I'm so sorry."

"There's nothing to apologize for," I said. "It's absolutely okay."

Then he asked, "Can I have another hug?"

"Sure." Another hug.

His friend joined, and suddenly we were in a group hug on

my sidewalk, laughing, crying, hugging—this beautiful reunion in the heart.

When it ended, we wiped our tears, looked at each other one last time, and they turned and walked away side by side—two embodiments of love.

I stood there, tears of gratitude streaming down my cheeks for this reunion in the heart. So grateful for all the practices that let the love we are be liberated. Without them, I'd still be holding onto my rightness. I'd have missed this. I probably would've run the other way. I'm so thankful for these practices—especially the Loving Blessing Practice—that allow us to live as this love.

THE POWER OF THE LOVING BLESSING PRACTICE

LET'S EXPLORE THE POWER OF THE LOVING BLESSING PRACTICE—
the same practice we touched on in the last chapter, first introduced to me during my summer at the ashram in 1998.

In Sanskrit, it's called *Ashirwad*, which means letting the
love that we are be shared as a blessing. It's an ancient practice,
shared down through the ages for thousands of years—a very
powerful, simple, and beautiful way to allow this love that we
are to flow to others.

In this practice, we become aware of someone—a person,
an animal, even a flower—anything that lets us easily feel
unconditional love. For me, it was often one of my sons who
would naturally arise in my awareness. Then we simply share,
beam, or emanate this love to them. This is the first stage of the
Loving Blessing Practice.

If, while doing this, someone else arises in awareness—
someone we might struggle to share love with—we don't judge
it. We just gently return to that being we can easily love and
begin again. Over time, it builds a momentum. It's a beautiful
practice.

That summer, I was so moved by it that I entered into the

Loving Blessing Practice every day. It became a consistent start to my days, continuing through summer, into fall, and then into winter. By winter, I learned there would be a live broadcast from the ashram of a day-long chanting meditation—a closed-circuit broadcast to various places around the world. Denver, Colorado, where I lived, was one of them. So I attended.

As the broadcast began, I was tender—seeing the ashram again on screen, the grounds and people and buildings that had meant so much to me. During the event, someone I'd met there the previous summer came strongly into my awareness. She was a friend of my son's who had often joined us at meals —a kind, delightful soul that we got to know well. I didn't know where she was—at the ashram again, home, or somewhere else in the world—but it didn't matter. In the Loving Blessing Practice, you don't have to know where someone is. You simply hold them in awareness and let the love you are be shared as a blessing.

So that day, as I watched the broadcast, I kept sending her love, over and over. If I drifted, I brought myself back, continuing to let this love be shared with her. It felt so natural and peaceful, like we were somehow together in that love.

At the end of the event, I called her to see how she was doing.

When she answered, she said, "Mitch, I'm so glad you called. I have to tell you what happened today."

She explained that she'd been out for a walk by the lake at the ashram that morning, feeling so sad she couldn't take part in the live broadcast. She didn't know I was watching it in Denver.

Then she said, "Suddenly, you came into my awareness. It was like you were comforting me—hugging me, telling me everything was going to be okay. I felt so much joy. I decided to go sign up for the day-long event. I even looked around for you, wondering if you might be there. Later, as I was sitting in the chanting, it felt like you were right beside me, holding my hand. My heart opened up so fully to a level of love that was indescribable. I was so grateful for your presence. It felt like you were with me all day long, and that we did in fact experience the day-long event together—even though your body wasn't here."

Then she paused. "Oh, I totally interrupted you. Why did you call me?"

I shared with her that all day long, I had been sending her love in the Loving Blessing Practice.

That moment revealed to me, so clearly, the real power of this practice. Even without knowing, she felt it. The love that we are is energetically shared—instantly, effortlessly. She was open enough to feel it, even to recognize it was me.

This is the true wonder of the Loving Blessing Practice. Every time we do it, not only do we get to experience the love that we are, ever more liberated, but the one we share it with also receives it and benefits from it. In every moment, we can let ourselves be available to an animal or a person or a flower, or anyone or anything that allows us to feel unconditional love, and we can let this unconditional, absolute love that we are be shared as a blessing.

LOVING BLESSING PRACTICE

AFTER READING THROUGH THIS PRACTICE, WE INVITE YOU TO experience it directly. The Loving Blessing Practice is available as a guided audio on the *Wanter Dynamics & The Love We Are Podcast,* accessible on all major streaming platforms, YouTube, and at TheLoveWeAre.com.

I invite you to bring your attention to your breath. Let your breath naturally begin to elongate—each in-breath nice and long and slow, each out-breath nice and long and slow. Feel your whole body relax as you breathe this way.

Now, allow someone or something to come into your awareness that you can feel unconditional love toward. It could be a person, an animal, a flower—anything that helps you get in touch with that pure, unconditional love. Let yourself feel that love. Really get in touch with it.

Now allow yourself to share that love, emanate that—like a fountain of that love. Just shower that person, that animal, or that thing with absolute love. Beam that love freely. Notice this love that you are. That's your True Nature. Notice how this love doesn't need to be thanked. It doesn't need to be returned. It doesn't require validation or confirmation. It has no needs at all. It's simply pure, unconditional love—no constraints, no requirements.

Feel how naturally it flows from you. That is what you are: love that gives freely, with no conditions.

Continue beaming this love, feeling its natural fullness—no conditions, no requirements. You've always been this love, and you always will be. Absolutely.

As you continue letting this love emanate, see if someone else you know comes into your awareness. Allow yourself to shower them with this same love. Notice what that feels like.

If someone comes in and you notice it's more difficult to beam them this love, that's perfectly okay. No judgment. Just return to your original person or object of origin—back to where unconditional love flows most easily, and begin again. Beam the love that you are.

As this practice continues, whoever comes into your awareness becomes part of the exploration. Sometimes, someone appears and the love contracts—we feel justified in withholding the love. These are choice points. In these moments, we can either hold on to the list of grievances that justify withholding love, or we can let it go. That's the choice. If we can't let it go right now, that's okay. No judgment. Just return to your point of origin—beaming love where it flows freely. Over time, this builds momentum. Eventually, people who once caused contraction will come into your awareness, and you'll find you can extend love to them too.

What we start to see is that when we choose to hold on—choosing to be right—we don't get to be free. We get to be right, but we don't get to be love. There comes a point where we're less interested in being right, and more interested in being love. Then, the love is liberated.

So we return to this practice again and again—allowing the

love that we are to flow, returning back to where it flows most easily whenever it contracts, never judging ourselves. This is how the love that we are becomes ever more free, eventually flowing toward all beings. That is the profound potential of what we truly are: love, completely liberated toward everyone and everything.

This is the freedom. This is the lovely possibility.

You are that love. You always have been—and you always will be.

ENJOYING THE RIDE

I RECENTLY COMPLETED A FLOW WITH SOMEONE I'VE BEEN exploring with for many years. She shared that she's noticing how often she can now interact with other humans more from True Nature; she's not so easily pulled in and captured by her Wanter. She reflected on how much easier it all feels when we're in our true essence, rather than caught in The Wanter. She shared that in many situations, she's naturally able to meet people with understanding, kindness, and patience—without needing them to be different than they are.

Then she asked me, "In the really tricky moments, how do you navigate those?"

I told her, "Over the years, I've found that moment to moment, I bring all my attention into the heart center within my body. I say, *Please let me be love.* I align with love. I let my choice be love. What I've learned is that when we let the choice be love, we're free. Whatever then arises from within my heart center, I do my best to let that be how I meet the person in that moment."

She paused and said, "Wow. So you align with love."

I said, "That is the lovely possibility."

"But what about the really tricky situations?" she asked.

What instantly came to mind was the retired airline captain. As you may recall, there's a sharing where I tell that whole story—you can refer back to that if you'd like. It's a good example of a truly tricky moment. Because when he arrived, he didn't want to be there. He was deep in his Wanter, and the first thing he did was try to crush my hand with a very firm hand- shake. Right then, I dropped into the heart center: *Please let me be love.* And in that moment, my arm muscles flexed, and I squeezed his hand firmly back—and he released. That's what love looked like then.

If that energy had words, it might have said: *Come on now, I love you too much to let you hurt me. We can do better than this.*

The love that I am wasn't going to let him harm me—that, too, was love expressing itself. From there, we went on. There were many tricky moments with him.

She said, "Wow, there's no way I could do that with someone trying to hurt me."

I told her, "The only reason that could happen for me is because of all the years of practice: Name That Thought, Problem Solver Mind, First Growl, Living Practice, Loving Blessing, and Chanting."

Eventually, we become more stabilized. We live more from our true essence, which is patient, kind, loving, agile—able to navigate tricky moments like that. With the retired airline captain, the Loving Blessing Practice was so essential. Because the more we're in that practice, the more we directly experience the love that we are—love that so naturally shares itself. The love we are, loves.

She then told me she's noticing how hard it is to share love with some people in her life, but how easy it is to share the love with her dog. I smiled. Over the years I've seen that for so many; the easiest being to help us touch the absolute love that we are is a pet. Very often, a dog. It's almost always a dog that people start the Loving Blessing Practice with.

Why is it so easy to feel unconditional love toward dogs? Look at how unconditionally loving they are. They wag their tails, snuggle in, so happy to see us—like we're the most important person that's ever existed. It feels so good to be loved that way. And yet, dogs still do dog things. They chew up furniture, make messes—things we'd rather they didn't do. But we let them off the hook. Why? Because we know they can only operate inside the construct of being a dog. We don't expect them to do more than what dogs are capable of.

The question then becomes: could we let The Wanter off the hook in the same way? Because when someone's in their Wanter, they're going to do Wanter things—just like dogs do dog things. The difference is, we often get upset at people when they do Wanter things, whereas we understand it with dogs. What if we could see: whenever anyone is captured in their Wanter, there's actually an opportunity for compassion. It doesn't mean we condone harmful behavior. Wanters can do very unkind things: be mean, manipulative, controlling, even betray or harm. Those are not aligned with True Nature. They're always selfish, caring only for themselves.

We're not saying such behavior is lovely, it's not. But when someone's in their Wanter, that's what shows up. If we understand this, it changes how we relate to people. The more we practice—especially the Loving Blessing Practice—the more we become stabilized in the love that we are. That love becomes ever more liberated. Then, when we're with someone in a very tricky moment, we can keep aligning: *Please let me be love.* Over and over. If we're truly stabilized in the love that we are, we won't be so upset at them for being in their Wanter. We can see it, have compassion, and just be with them right where they are.

What often happens is they begin to relax back into their

own True Nature. That's what happened with the retired airline captain. By the end of that first session, he was more in his heart. I didn't have that as an agenda—it was simply a lovely possibility. Same with the story of walking with the Mormons that I share in "Liberating This Love We Are." It was all those years of Loving Blessing that allowed me to meet them that way —so many years later, on a walk in my neighborhood. On that walk with the Mormons, we all shared a beautiful reunion in the heart.

When we do this, we no longer need people to be different. They're let off the hook, like the doggy friends. We stay wise— we don't put ourselves in danger. But we also stay in love, without an agenda, just by abiding in who we really are.

This love that we are can be liberated. We can meet others from this truth. So when she asked me how to navigate the tricky moments, I told her: it's always moment to moment, resting into the heart center, saying: *Please let me be love. Please let me be love.*

Because when we let the choice be love, we are free. And it's so much easier to enjoy the ride.

LOVING THE LITTLE ONE ORIGINS

WE ALL HAVE WITHIN US A LITTLE FRAGILE ONE—VERY YOUNG and insecure. That little one in all of us feels unworthy and unloved and lonely, and longs for unconditional love that's reliable and dependable and will bring comfort to us when we're feeling those kinds of feelings. This is very normal in our human experience.

When that part of us gets triggered and we're feeling like that, I have, over the years, invited people into a practice that came to me one night, which I call the Loving the Little One practice, where we let ourselves honor that little one inside of us.

I invite people to let an image of their little one come into their awareness: What are they wearing? What's their hair like? How old are they? What are they feeling? I invite people to honor that little one who's feeling lonely, or sad, or insecure, or unlovable, or unwanted. Then, we let the big love that we are, be brought to our little one—to bring comfort to our little one. It has been very beneficial for many people for many years. That practice came to me one night, many years ago, in a very unexpected and surprising way.

I had been doing the Loving Blessing Practice for many years prior to that night. In the Loving Blessing practice, we let someone come into our awareness and we share the love we are with that person. We honor them, and let the love we are be shared with them. On the particular evening I'm referring to, I had gotten home late from a full day at the studio, had a late dinner, and sat down to watch a movie. After a little bit of time watching the movie, I could feel—behind me and to my right in the kitchen—the potato chips in my cabinet calling to me: *We're crunchy. We're salty. Come eat us.* The craving—something that had happened so often in my journey prior to that evening —arose again. Of course, it's something that happens for all of us: for our Wanter.

As I was feeling this craving for the potato chips, I was aware that so many times in my journey The Wanter would win. I would get up and go get that bag of chips. Of course, it wouldn't be a single-serving bag. It would be one of those family-size bags of chips—a way too big for any human-size bag of chips. It would end up on my lap, and I would be eating them one after another as I watched the movie. All those calories your body does not need at eleven-thirty at night.

On this night, I wondered if the Living Practice would be useful for cravings. It had never even occurred to me to consider that. But on that evening, it did. *I wonder if the Living Practice would be beneficial regarding this craving?* As soon as I wondered it, I decided to attempt to use the Living Practice regarding the food craving.

I could feel my Wanter had no interest in this—*No, no Living Practice. Just get up out of this chair, go get that bag of chips, and let's have some comfort. Let's have some salt and some crunch. We want that.* I could feel my Wanter really had no interest in this spiritual practice mumbo jumbo. *Just get up and get those chips.* But somehow, through all the years of practice, there was enough curiosity that I stayed in my chair. The Wanter didn't win that night.

I began to notice: *Where do you feel this in your body?* As I turned my attention to where I was feeling the craving, I assumed it was going to be in my stomach. To my surprise, the energy was not in my stomach—it was in my heart. That was so surprising to me!

As I went right into that feeling in my heart, I became aware that what was really going on was loneliness. I just felt so lonely. I wasn't expecting that. It turns out that's what was underneath the craving for the potato chips. I realized in that moment—wow—this has been the source of my cravings all along. Underneath it was loneliness. My Wanter had come up with the strategy of going to get something to snack on, to bring some comfort to the discomfort. It was a strategy of my Wanter to try to make things better for me. I realized my whole life, that's where that late-night snacking was coming from—feeling lonely.

I was so grateful to my Wanter in that moment for how often it had tried to bring comfort to that loneliness. Of course, I was also aware that it had never worked. It would only bring a temporary comfort to this feeling, but it wouldn't actually address what was underneath it.

So, as I stayed with it, and stayed with it, and stayed with it, all of a sudden I saw a little, young version of me—a little three-year-old me. A little guy, with little jeans on, and little tennis shoes, and a little T-shirt, and a haircut that back in those days was called a crew cut, where your hair was cut really short. Little blonde hair, little blue-eyed, little. He was feeling so alone, and so sad, and so wanting to feel love. He was feeling so alone.

Right in that moment, I could feel how much I understood him and how much I love him unconditionally. I could feel this big love and compassion flow right to him and hug him. It was like the Loving Blessing Practice for my little one. After all those years of Loving Blessing Practice—it so easily flowed right into my little guy, my little three-year-old Mitchie.

I hugged him and honored him and let him know, "Everything's okay. I'm right here with you. You don't have to in any way change how you're feeling. You don't need to stop feeling how you're feeling. You get to feel exactly how you're feeling. I love you without any requirements, without any conditions. This love that I bring to you has no limits, will never run out, will never betray you, will never abandon you, will never in any way have any agenda towards you at all. Absolute, reliable, dependable, trustworthy, unconditional love."

It was amazing. My little one turned right toward that inner love and melted right into that loving embrace. I realized in that moment—all these years, these cravings were coming from my little one who was feeling lonely. This love allowed my little one to rest so completely into that love and he melted into that loving embrace.

I let my little one know, "Anytime you feel this way, you can turn toward this love that I am, that I bring to you. It will always be here for you. You can always find it here. This is the love that will always be true and available to you, without any limits or requirements." He rested right into that.

All my life I had had this feeling and had been looking for love outside, from someone else. I realized then, that the only love that can truly bring this little one into rest, is this inner, absolutely reliable, unconditional love.

This is a lovely possibility—that each of us can let ourselves be available to this practice: Loving the Little One Practice. Anything in our lived life that triggers this insecurity, this loneliness, this unworthiness feeling. We can turn within, become aware of our little one, and let the love that we are be shared.

Our little one will, through this practice, eventually realize that it can always turn within for this love, and that this love will be reliable and dependable and unconditional.

LOVING THE LITTLE ONE PRACTICE

AFTER READING THROUGH THIS PRACTICE, WE INVITE YOU TO experience it directly. The Loving The Little One Practice is available as a guided audio on the *Wanter Dynamics & The Love We Are Podcast,* accessible on all major streaming platforms, YouTube, and at TheLoveWeAre.com.

Here we are, this love all together, lovely.

It's so easy to lose touch with that inherent essence within us. As we journey in these lives, we experience certain events that hurt our feelings. Maybe a moment where we find out we weren't invited to the party that everyone else was invited to. There may be a moment where we're not included on the playground. When we're little, there may be a moment where we're the new kid at school in the cafeteria that first day, holding our tray, and there isn't anyone who's welcoming us or inviting us to come sit at their table.

There may be moments where we're in a group gathering and we seem to be the only one that other people are not paying attention to. There can be moments where we're not invited to go on the trip that all the other friends we know, were invited to go on. There are all kinds of life events where we get left out, where we don't matter, where we're not cared for, where we're cast aside.

In those moments, there's a possibility to face that disturbance—what it triggers within us—that core belief that we're not wanted, that we don't matter, that we're unworthy. Unwantable. It can spiral all the way into that place where we believe we're just unwantable, unlovable.

When that happens, there's a way that I've explored over the years in my own journey–and with all the people that I've had the great honor of exploring the nature of reality with–that we can, if we're willing, turn within. Rather than trying to compensate, distract, or move away from the discomfort—which is usually our instinct—there's another possibility. We can let go of the strategies we've picked up over time: stuffing it down, avoiding it, or getting so lost in it that we can't get out of bed. Instead of being pulled into depression or swallowed by the feeling, we allow ourselves to face it directly. Instead of all that, another lovely possibility is to simply stop, turn our attention within, and become aware of this little one in us—that little one that feels alone. In those moments, if we turn within, sometimes we'll become aware of a younger, earlier version of ourselves. Sometimes you'll even get a little imagery of that little one—a certain moment in time where we remember being left out.

I invite people to go back to the earliest moments they remember ever feeling cast aside, left out, or unwanted—and try to remember what age they were. I'll often invite people to let an image come. I'll say, "I invite you to close your eyes and just turn within. When was the earliest experience that you remember being left out, feeling alone, unwanted, undesirable, like you didn't matter?"

If you'd like, you can recall your earliest memories of your journey with your eyes closed, just turning within, letting your breath be a little bit longer and slower. In a very courageous, willing way, let yourself recall those early experiences and see if an image comes of yourself at the earliest moment.

I invite you to notice: What were you wearing? What was your hairdo, your outfit, your environment? Let that image come to you, whatever that is. Let yourself become aware of that little version of you. All the details—the clothing you were wearing, what your hair was like, if you had glasses or not. Whatever it was like for you in that moment, let that little one be in your awareness. Let yourself *see* that little one.

Now notice how there's this awareness—that *you* are in this moment—that's very much aware of that little version of you and understands that little version of you completely, with absolute compassion. Let that absolute compassion—that loving awareness—just very naturally be brought to this little version of you. Just a pure, loving embrace with complete understanding. Complete acceptance. Letting this little version of you know that they get to be just how they are. They don't have to change. They don't need to be different than they are. They get to be just how they are right now. Letting the breath be nice and long and slow, we're just bringing unconditional loving acceptance to this little one in us. Allowing our little one to be completely and unconditionally loved and honored and accepted.

This *you* that's aware of that little version of you completely understands and brings absolute love, brings that loving embrace. Letting this little one know that they can be exactly how they are. They don't have to be different than they are. That little version of you gets to be just how it is. Doesn't have to change, doesn't have to be worthy of this love, doesn't have to earn the love, doesn't have to be better, doesn't have to in any way feel different than that little one feels. We're just letting that little one be honored and embraced, completely accepted.

Let this little one be completely and naturally at rest in this love. This little one can receive this love. We can let it be known to our little one that this love is reliable, dependable, and will never betray or abandon. This is a love that the little one can always rely on, and will always be dependable. There isn't anything that has to be done by the little one to earn the love—completely and naturally. This is a love that will always be there for your little one. Resting in that. Fully embracing this little one with this absolute, unconditional loving acceptance—pure compassion, pure kindness, a loving embrace—and our little one can rest now in that love.

We allow this direct experience of this pure love being brought to our little one. What we will begin to notice is: the love that we're bringing to our little one *is what we always will be.* This little one that we're honoring is a memory from previous experiences. What we really are—we start to realize in this practice—is the love that we bring to our little one. We are this love that is forever.

You'll always be this love. Notice how this love that you are, that you bring, doesn't need to be loved back, doesn't need to be validated or confirmed or honored or thanked. This love is without conditions, and *you are this love* that has no conditions, no constraints, no limits. Letting yourself feel this love that you bring to your little one.

In these moments, when anything happens in life where our little one gets activated and is feeling sad and unwanted, we just bring the love to our little one, honoring this loving embrace. Little by little, what happens is, this little one in us starts to rest into that love, starts to in some ways dissolve or melt into the love. The little one just starts to rest into the love. We start to realize: We *are* this love, we've always been this love, and we will always be this love.

Notice the simple, elegant wholeness of this love that you are, that you've always been, that so naturally and so compassionately and with such patience and understanding, loves our little one—no matter what it is that triggered it. Whatever life situation triggers this—where we feel sad, or alone, or unwanted—we can turn within and bring love to our little one.

What we start to realize is: we are the love that we bring to the little one. No matter how many times that little one got loved by someone else, it was never enough. Our little one will always need more external love. The external love from someone else won't ever bring this little one in us to rest. The only way that this little one rests is when *we* bring this inner love to our little one. We start to realize that *we* are this inner love. We've always been this love. And this love is without conditions, without constraints, without limit. We can rest in that love that we are—that loving acceptance, that wisdom, that clarity, that naturalness that we are.

Expand out into that love. Notice that love that you are—that acceptance, that naturalness, that beingness that you are. Notice it doesn't end at the edge of your body. Roam out, out, out beyond your body. Notice it is without edges, without boundaries—this love that you are is absolute. You've always been this, and you will always be this.

Rest out now into the stillness of this love. The absoluteness of this love that you are, that you've always been, and that you will always be. Your breath can be longer and slower. Here we are, this love, all together, lovely.

THE LOVELY POSSIBILITY OF CHANTING

SOUND—THE VIBRATION OF ENERGY AT VARYING FREQUENCIES— has an effect on matter, because matter itself is also a vibration. Everything in existence is a vibration. Even something that appears to be really solid, like a block of marble, steel, titanium, or gold, seems so dense that you wouldn't imagine it's vibrating. But everything is a vibrational occurrence in this reality. So, sound affects things. This has been scientifically proven.

Chanting is the repetitive vocalization of sounds or phrases, often creating a rhythmic and vibrational experience. When it comes to chanting, what we notice is that there are certain melodies, certain frequencies, certain combinations of sounds that have a beneficial effect on our human body. Throughout human history, we have let ourselves be available to rhythms and sounds. Some feel really resonant in our bodies, while others feel more dissonant. The lovely possibility of chanting is that we let ourselves be immersed in a vibrational field that is very beneficial to the energy systems of the body.

There are natural ways of chanting that help open us into a larger perspective, where we are more likely to experience the interconnectivity of reality, the inherent unity of existence.

When we chant, it opens up the energy channels in the body and tends to quiet the mind, because the chanting I am referring to is energetic. It is like being inside of a circle. The chants go round and round, like being inside a giant three-dimensional sphere, all circular, all encompassing. So the mind tends to become more quiet as we let ourselves be available to these pure sounds.

Throughout history, the truly ancient spiritual lineages always had some sort of rhythmic, circular chanting. It allows the mind to relax, to soften. We become less identified with experiencing reality through the perspective of the mind, and more open to the perspective of our eternal true essence. Chanting is a very powerful spiritual practice. When I was at the ashram, a large percentage of our daily schedule included chanting as the main practice we would enter into in various ways.

When I was a little guy, my mom and I played with sound. She called it the "song game." Whatever melody was coming to her—maybe a popular song on the radio or a nursery rhyme—we would play a song game where she would let spontaneous words come to the melody, related to whatever we were experiencing. Then she would look at me, and I could tell it was my turn. It was a sort of call and response. She would get the song started, and we would flow in a circle together, round and round, and play.

We let ourselves play in sound, in melodies, with words that would arrive in the melodies. Sometimes the words wouldn't fit, and we would laugh and be silly and let ourselves play. Chanting is a really natural way to let ourselves play in melodies. Very often, when we let ourselves play in melody, we can feel the body wanting to move and dance and express itself. The body is affected by sound. When we let ourselves chant, we can open to the giggly one within us, the dancing one, the playful one.

We start to discover that we don't actually have a problem here. We open into the perspective of the adventure of this human life, rather than being stuck in our problem-solver mind and our Wanter, where the perspective is that everything is a problem, where everything is very serious. When we dance and sing and play, we find our way to that natural playful one that we are, the one filled with wonder and available to the adventure.

We inevitably come to the natural realization through our direct experience when we chant that we don't have a problem here. This is the lovely possibility when we let ourselves chant. We naturally find our way to to who we are, that is so playful, so wise, so capable of experiencing life from the perspective that the whole thing, no matter what's occurring, is an adventure.

This is the lovely possibility of chanting, and I am so honored to share these chants with you that have come to me over the years. They are a combination of English and Sanskrit. Any of the Sanskrit words you hear will always be referring to something very lovely.

For example, there is *ananda*, which means the bliss of the divine play of consciousness.

There is *jivan*, which means your human experience, your lived human life.

There is *jivanmukti*, which means liberation from limiting thoughts and beliefs, liberation from the illusion of separation, and together it reveals the lovely possibility of being liberated while still living in this body.

There is *om*, the sound of the universe, the vibration of everything.

There is *namah*, which means I bow, I let go, I welcome, I release into.

There is *Shiva*, a Sanskrit word that refers to our true essence, the essence that permeates all reality.

There is *sat*, which means the eternal existing truth of existence. *Chit*, which means pure consciousness, pure awareness; and again, *ananda*, bliss, ease, contentment.

So *sat chitananda* means we are that which eternally exists, inherently pure consciousness, aware and at ease, and blissful.

Sometimes you will hear *namo namah* combined together, meaning I bow, I release the need for control, I let go into the unknown, I honor and welcome the mystery.

You may also hear *Shakti* or *Chiti Shakti*, which is another way of referring to the absolute flowing essence that permeates all reality.

All of these Sanskrit terms point to something very lovely about the eternal truth of our absolute, eternal loveliness. As you let yourself be available to these melodies, these playful, fun chants, you'll hear lots of moments where I have a mess-up and just start giggling. All of this is the natural way of these recordings—very playful, very fun, very real, raw, open, silly, and playful.

I am honored to share them with you. When we let ourselves play, we find our way. This is the lovely possibility of chanting.

If you'd like to explore chanting more deeply, complete playlists are available at TheLoveWeAre.com.

A PLAYGROUND IN THE MIRROR

I INVITE YOU TO IMAGINE THAT YOU BRING A FULL-BODY-LENGTH mirror to a playground. You prop it up and look into the mirror, seeing everything reflected in it in this playground environment. You see the slide, the swing set, the monkey bars, the children playing, people walking through the park with their dogs, people playing catch with a Frisbee, someone flying a kite, people having picnics out on the grass, as you look further out into the park beyond the playground.

While staying really focused on all of the objects appearing in the mirror—at some point, you could start to believe that all of those objects are somehow separate things occurring. You could lose track of the mirror, when the ultimate truth is: there's only the mirror. It is all occurring in the mirror. Every person, every swing set, every monkey bar, every dog, every Frisbee, every picnic, every tree, every blade of grass, every flower, every bush—there's only the mirror.

If we let this be a metaphor for reality: there's only *Chiti*, a Sanskrit word for the Source Essence of everything. In the same way that there's only the mirror, and all of the objects appearing in the mirror are reflections occurring in it, there's only *Chiti*. No matter how believable all these objects look to us, there's only the mirror. In the same way, there's only *Chiti*. Everything that occurs in this realm is a reflection and expression of that. It's all occurring in *Chiti*.

When I invite you into the Name That Thought Practice, I invite you to be on the lookout—to see if a thought comes to your mind. If so, we honor the thought. We honor the mind—that's what the mind does; it thinks thoughts. We name the thought. It's like naming what's appearing in the mirror 'thought.' Then we rest back, being available for the possibility of another reflection to appear—another thought. If one arises, we name that thought, honor it, and rest back again. What am I inviting you to rest back into? That which you eternally, always are: your mirror nature—pure witness consciousness. Everything is occurring in the awareness that you are. That's your *Chiti* nature. You are the mirror in which every thought is occurring. The thoughts are occurring in the awareness that you are.

If we get pulled into the thought and identified with it, it can lead to another one, and another, and then all kinds of emotional disturbances can unfold. We become completely captured by that object in the mirror of consciousness—believing that we are this separate someone who needs things to be different than they are. From there, all the suffering, the stories, and everything else unfolds. There's nothing wrong with that. That's part of the realm we're exploring. We do tend to get captured—that's what mostly happens. We get identified as the object in the mirror, when all along, we are still the mirror.

If we let the mirror continue to be the metaphor for awareness—consciousness, *Chiti*—each time you name the thought in the Name That Thought Practice, I'm inviting you to rest back into witness consciousness. Pure awareness that you are —that the thought is occurring in—rather than getting identified as the thought that's occurring in the awareness that you are.

In the Name That Thought Practice, you're invited to rest back into the awareness and not get pulled into that thought. That might be a thought of, *I'm not good enough*, or *it matters what other people think, I need someone's validation, I need to make sure that they like me.* All those plays of our Wanter and our Problem Solver Mind—those are all occurring in the awareness, the infinite eternal awareness that you are.

Let's say we start to get pulled into a thought and we start to worry. Let's say we start to get pulled into some forward Problem Solver Mind—going forward-in-time type thought—trying to solve something that might be a problem. Let's say we get captured. That's okay if we do. That's part of what we're exploring here. We *do* get captured, and we start to worry. Right in that moment, we have the Problem Solver Mind Practice, where, if you can catch it early and say, "Hey, Problem Solver Mind, is there anything of benefit that needs to be done right now regarding that?" The answer will be no, because it's forward of this moment. Then we thank our Problem Solver Mind: "Thank you, Problem Solver Mind, for always trying to solve every potential problem for me. You're always looking out for me. Thank you so much." Then I invite you to focus on long, slow breath, and then rest back into pure awareness again.

Let's say we can't catch it at the Name That Thought Practice. We can't catch it at the Problem Solver Mind Practice. Then we have First Growl Practice. Now you're starting to get really affected. It's starting to pull you in. You're starting to have a disturbance—what I refer to as a growl. First Growl Practice: as soon as you feel that, stop and ask, "What is my Wanter wanting that it's not getting?" This once again allows us to rest back into witness consciousness, our mirror nature in which that disturbance is occurring. We are the awareness in which that is occurring. So we can thank our Wanter: "Thank you so much, Wanter, for wanting it to be different than it is—wanting it to not be raining on my picnic that I planned here today in this park. Thank you so much for wanting that for me. You're right. It would be way better for me if it wasn't raining on my picnic. But now I'm going to focus on long, slow breath."

When we're focusing on the long, slow breath, we're not getting pulled back into the suffering. Long, slow breath relaxes our nervous system—allows us to relax back into our mirror nature, pure awareness. Then we're no longer upset about the rain. We're now in acceptance of the rain, and we navigate accordingly. Maybe we decide to have a: *Let's dance in the rain* flow. Who knows. How we would play is different when we're resting back into the larger perspective that all of this is occurring in what we are. There's no actual separation; there's only *Chiti*, and we are that—and so is the rain, and so is our picnic that's getting all wet, and so is that dog, and so is that Frisbee, and so are those monkey bars, and so is that cloud, and so is that building, and so is that tree, and so is that flower.

Now, let's say we can't catch a disturbance at Name That Thought Practice. We can't catch it at Problem Solver Mind Practice. We didn't catch it at the First Growl, and now we're just *in*. Sometimes it's so quick—you're just *in*. You're just disturbed. You're affected. There's emotion going on. We're so frustrated about this rain that's happening.

At that moment, there's now a possibility of the Living Practice. In the Living Practice, I invite you to notice: where are you feeling this in your body? Maybe it's in the heart center. We're just heartbroken. We're so upset that this picnic we planned for three months is getting rained out. What do we do? We honor the feeling. Where do you feel this in your body? You feel it right there in your heart center. Just let yourself experience that. We're honoring that.

What is that? That is also *Chiti*. It's a contraction of *Chiti*, because something's not going how we want it to go. That's what contracts the field energy—whenever things don't go how we want them to go, how our Wanter wants them to go. It contracts the field energy. We're now honoring that in our heart center. We allow it to be directly experienced. Then, once you're really letting it be experienced without any agenda— we're not trying to figure it out or solve it or change it or fix it— we're just letting it be directly experienced.

Then I always invite people to notice, once you're really letting yourself experience this—that is also *Chiti*, the contraction of *Chiti*—notice it's not all that you are, because you're also the awareness of this contracted *Chiti* flow. You're also pure witness consciousness in which this is occurring within your heart center, within your body. You are the awareness in which that disturbance is occurring—in the heart center, in the body —and all of that. The disturbance, the heart center in your body, and your body are all occurrences within the vast field of awareness that you are.

That's why, at that point, I invite you to notice, this isn't all you are—what you're feeling in your body—because you're also the awareness of it, and it's actually in the awareness that you are that this occurrence is rising up in. When we're in that perspective, what we notice is the contracted *Chiti* energy uncontracts in its own time. As long as we have no agenda, it will uncontract all on its own. Now we're resting back into that which we eternally are—this vast awareness that we are in which that disturbance was occurring within the heart center of the body—and all of that is occurring in *Chiti* that you are.

The Loving Blessing Practice. I invite you to let either an animal or a person come into your awareness that you can feel unconditional love toward, you let that love be shared with that other being. You're now directly experiencing the characteristic of this witness consciousness that you are, which is pure love. The love that you then share—to that dog, that cat, that person, whatever is your being of origin that you can feel unconditional love toward—that love is the essence of the witness consciousness. The essence of the mirror is absolute love. We are a pure awareness that is inherently unconditionally loving.

In the Loving Blessing Practice, we share that love. You get to directly experience that the love that you are is not only a noun; it's also a verb. The love that we are loves without any conditions—another way of resting in your True Nature, your *Chiti* nature. Pure awareness that's aware of the being that we've brought into awareness, and then the love that we are—that we then share—that emanates from us in the same way that the rays of the sun naturally emanate. The rays of the sun are like the love that we are. We are the sun, and we are also the love. We are the awareness, and we are also the love.

Chanting. When we chant, it vibrationally tunes the energy centers in the body, allowing them to open more easily to a larger perspective—that we are *Chiti*, pure awareness that is inherently loving. The vibration of the chant occurs within that field of awareness that we are. So we chant, round and round. The chants are like circles. We go round and round. These are non-linear vibrational invitations—the chants. We begin to experience reality in a non-linear way. We can open up into the eternal, infinite simplicity of existence—the simplicity of eternal existence.

Within this metaphor of the mirror, everything occurring in the mirror—though it may appear to be separate, because it's such a compelling image—is still only the mirror. In the same way, we are *Chiti*, absolute Source Essence, and everything that occurs is a reflection happening within *Chiti*. It's all real. Every reflection is real. Every human life, every movement of the mind, the emotions, the interactions, the moment-to-moment experiences—they're all real. And they're all temporary vibrations, risings and fallings of *Chiti*. Everything is an expression of *Chiti*. If we return to our mirror metaphor—it's always occurring in the mirror, and it's always *Chiti*.

From this perspective, we realize: we don't have a problem here. The whole of it—all of it—is a play, an adventure, in which it's possible to become so captured and misidentified with all kinds of experiences of separation and suffering, The Wanter, the growling, and all of that. But none of that is wrong or bad. That is the divine play.

Then, inevitably, we begin to notice this mystery, become available to it, wonder about it, explore it—and we find our way to invitations. All of the practices I've invited you into are simply that: invitations to experience for yourself.

The true lineages are never about being asked to *believe* something. They are about untangling from beliefs and being invited into direct experience. It is in direct experience that the Truth is revealed.

VIVEKA

Let's explore *Viveka*. *Viveka* is a Sanskrit word. If we transliterate it from Sanskrit into English, we could say that it means *refined discernment*. It's a practice that we were invited into at the ashram.

The wisdom of this practice—and its inherent invitation—is to notice, in every moment when we're making a choice or decision, that whatever we choose will have corresponding ripples. In the practice of *Viveka*, there are two aspects: *Shreyas* and *Preyas*. As we enter into this practice, we will not overlay any constructs of good and bad, right and wrong onto it. That isn't part of the invitation.

In this practice, it's simply choice. There isn't a right choice or a wrong choice, a good choice or a bad choice. There is simply choice—and whatever we choose will bring the consequences or ripples that follow that choice. If we choose *Shreyas*, those are the choices made from our true essence—choices that are truly beneficial for ourselves and others. These are choices that consider impact. Choices that are compassionate, kind, and loving. If we choose *Preyas* choices, they are temporarily pleasurable or stimulating—choices made to gain attention, approval, control, power, or manipulation. These are choices that come from the aspect of our human expression I call The Wanter.

Now remember, as we ease into the *Preyas* category, try not to make *Preyas* wrong or bad. It's simply another way of choice. In our human experience, we can choose *Preyas*. It's not wrong or bad, but it will have the ripples that come with it. If we betray someone to get ahead, that comes with *Preyas* ripples. If we harm, manipulate, or speak behind someone's back in a non-beneficial way, or engage in selfish activities—this is *Preyas*. These choices come with their own ripple effects.

As we enter into the practice of *Viveka*, refined discernment, we're invited to—if at all possible—bring awareness to the moment we're making a choice, and consider: Is this *Preyas* or is it *Shreyas*? It's that simple. It's not easy—but it is simple.

Let's look at an example. Let's say we're hungry, and one of our friends offers us something to eat. They invite us to sit at their table, they go into their kitchen, and return a bit later with two plates—one in each hand. They place them in front of us. On one plate is a big, triple-layer, mocha fudge, chocolatey chocolate cake with thick icing and a lot of sugar. On the other plate is organically grown, well-prepared, nicely steamed broccoli.

We now have a choice: we can eat the chocolate cake or the broccoli, but not both. For this example of *Viveka*, we must choose one or the other. In the practice of *Viveka*, we'd be invited to consider: Which one is *Shreyas*? Which one is *Preyas*?

Now, notice: in this practice, there's no construct that we *should* choose one or the other. There are no "shoulds." It's simply choice. One will be *Preyas*, and one will be *Shreyas*. We can imagine the big slice of chocolate cake doesn't have much nutritional value. It tastes sweet and yummy in the moment. Broccoli, on the other hand, offers our body wonderful nutritional benefits. In this example, choosing the broccoli would be *Shreyas* because it's beneficial to our body. Choosing the cake would be *Preyas* because it's temporarily pleasurable but may cause a sugar crash later, or digestive issues, especially if we're allergic to dairy. (For this example, let's say we're not allergic to broccoli.)

Again, in the practice of *Viveka*, one isn't *right* and the other *wrong*. One simply creates *Preyas* ripples, and the other creates *Shreyas* ripples. That's it. There is simply choice. There is that which is truly beneficial and that which is temporarily pleasurable. We're invited to notice cause and effect. That's all. Nowhere in this practice is there any orientation that one is better than the other. It's a practice of noticing that different types of choices bring different types of outcomes.

Now, what can be said—as someone who has been in the practice of *Viveka* for decades—is that you begin to notice *Preyas* choices more easily and become less interested in them. You become less likely to choose them because you've become aware of the complications and consequences they bring. You naturally begin to lean toward *Shreyas*. But in any given moment, we always have choice. There might be a day where I just want the chocolate cake. I choose to eat the cake instead of the broccoli. That's my choice.

In this beautiful practice, we remove all the overlays of good and bad, right and wrong, and simply notice: moment to moment, we make choices—and there will be corresponding ripples. If we choose *Preyas*, there will be *Preyas* ripples. If we choose *Shreyas*, there will be the ripples of *Shreyas*—beneficial, sustaining ripples.

This is the wonderful, playful way of *Viveka*: refined, very nuanced discernment.

SEVA

LET'S EXPLORE THE ANCIENT PRACTICE CALLED *SEVA*. IT transliterates into English as *selfless service*. When I spent all those years at the ashram, part of the daily schedule included doing some sort of activity every day to support the ashram. It was after lunch, two and a half to three hours, and it was one of the parts of a daily schedule, which started at 3:30 a.m. every day.

The daily schedule started with a morning *Āratī*, where you wave lights and sing a devotional Sanskrit chant, inviting in Grace. It begins there, with the morning *Āratī* at 3:30 a.m., and then throughout the day, there's a continual flow of various practices of chanting and meditation and learning. Ancient texts, even how you would have tea or have your meals, were all considered to be part of your *sadhana*. *Sadhana* is a Sanskrit word referring to your spiritual practices. Your spiritual life is your *sadhana*.

It was made very clear to us that it was all optional. You didn't have to do any of it. You could enter into the schedule anywhere you wanted. You didn't have to start at 3:30 a.m.; if you would rather jump into the schedule at 7:00 a.m. or 9:00

a.m., you could join in wherever you liked. Kind of like a river, we were invited to jump into the daily Schedule River wherever we liked each day.

All of it was optional, and the part of the schedule we're exploring here in this moment is in the afternoon, right after lunch, where you would be invited into a selfless service. They explained to us in our orientation that this was a practice that had been handed down for thousands of years as a way to let whatever work you do also be *sadhana*—your spiritual practice —where you let whatever it is you're doing be done non-egoically, selflessly, letting it be an offering to the community, to the wholeness of this sacred place. You're helping the place function and operate and keep the costs down, and everyone's pitching in and helping out.

The community aspect of Seva is where you're being available to the *we* aspect of reality, rather than the *me* aspect. Our Wanter is me-oriented, and our True Nature is we-oriented— where we're caring about the entire community. That doesn't leave us out either; when we're in the we, that also includes us. When we're in our Wanter, we're only doing it for ourselves. We're not caring about others.

In the practice of *Seva*, which transliterates into English as selfless service, that's the invitation. I was so inspired by this. I could see how this could translate and help me learn how to let all activities be done as Seva—selflessly, non-egoically.

My first day, it was after lunch and I realized it was time for *Seva*. So I was going to walk over to the building where they said you go to sign up for *Seva*. I was walking by the temple and saw that there were people already in there with these soft cloths, wiping down all the beautiful *murtis*, and the marble columns, in the nice air-conditioned temple.

Yes, yes, I'll do temple Seva. Yes! Because I love to be in the temple. That's where I go to meditate and chant and connect into my true self. Yes, that will give me even more time to be in the temple. I'll sign up for temple *Seva*.

I walk over to the other building to let them know I'll sign up for temple *Seva*. As I approached the table, the person there greets me and welcomes me with a big smile. They say to me, "Are you here to sign up for *Seva*?"

"Yes, absolutely," I said.

And right when I was going to tell her how willing and available I was to do temple *Seva*, I didn't get a chance to say anything. She reached into a box and pulled out a card.

I said, "What's that?"

She said, "This will be your *Seva* assignment."

"We don't get to choose our *Seva*?" I asked.

She giggled and said, "No, we assign you a *Seva* that's all coordinated, and we invite you, if you're willing, to do this Seva. Would you be willing to sign up for this?"

"Okay, sure." But there was a part of me a bit disappointed that I didn't get to choose *my Seva*. I wanted temple *Seva*. That's where I connect to the sacred, inside the temple. I want to do temple *Seva*. But I decided I was willing to roll with this. We'll see how it goes.

She handed me my card. It said on it: Housekeeping.

I said, "Housekeeping. What's that?"

She said, "If you go over to the other building called *Anugraha* and go down in the basement, there'll be a person there waiting to greet you and orient you to what part of house-keeping you'll be doing."

"Okay. Thank you." So I leave, holding my card that says Housekeeping.

During my walk, I wondered, "Okay, what could house-keeping be? Let's see—vacuuming, cleaning floors, sweeping, mopping?"

Then I arrive at the building, go down into the basement, and see a man standing by a supply cabinet and a woman standing there with him. You can tell they're waiting for me. I was a little bit late.

As I walk up, he says hello and tells me his name, and she says hello and tells me hers.

He said, "Welcome. So glad you're here. I'm so grateful that you're willing to do this *Seva*." He looked at both of us and said, "I just want to let both of you know that you've been given the most powerful *Seva* there is. The two of you will be cleaning toilets."

No.

First of all, I don't even like public restrooms to begin with, let alone be responsible for cleaning toilets. There was a part of me that wanted to run as fast as I could. *I don't want to do this Seva. I was fine doing temple Seva, the nice sacred air-conditioned, clean, beautiful temple. I'm not interested in toilet Seva.*

He went on to explain more of the details, and I could see the look on her face as well. I can't say for sure what she was experiencing, but it seemed like she was less than thrilled too. He explained that we would first chant a *mantra* in Sanskrit. He handed each of us a card and said, "Here's a card with the words in case you don't know the chant. We'll chant this, inviting in Grace to help us as best as we can not get pulled into that part of us that would resist, that would want it to not be occurring, that would want to be somewhere else. Instead, to align with the true spirit of *Seva*—selfless service—offering it to the community, to help the ashram operate and function. That this translates to our life. That this can be a way for us to learn how to let all our activities be a way of connecting to our heart essence, offering selflessly our activities into the world."

I could feel the invitation of this and really wanted to be in the spirit of it. So we chanted the opening mantra. I held my card, looking at the words, chanting this beautiful, simple, sweet melody. We invited in Grace, asked for support to stay in the true spirit of *Seva*, letting this be an offering to Grace, and to the community, in the most pure and beneficial way. We completed that, and he oriented us on the supplies: buckets, brushes, rubber gloves, and explained all the different buildings.

It was similar to a college campus, with a lot of buildings and distances between them. He said, "Mitch, you'll be doing all the men's restrooms in all of the buildings," and to her, "You'll be doing all the ladies' in all of the buildings." We had three hours to do all of this. He thanked us for our willingness to do the *Seva*, and then we began.

So I walked into the bathroom on that lower level in the basement to begin. I opened the door of the first stall, really trying to be in the spirit of *Seva*—selfless service. I was *sort of* in the spirit of it . . . not really, but I was trying to consider everything that is the spirit of *Seva*. Then I opened the door to the second stall. Still trying. And then I opened the door to the third stall and—*oh no*. I didn't even want to go into this stall. I didn't even want to approach this toilet, let alone be responsible for cleaning it. *No, no, no, no, no.*

Thus began my torturous relationship with toilet *Seva*. From that moment on, every toilet was just drudgery and a burden and unfair. *I've paid to come to this place, and now they've got me working here for free . . . not only for free, but I paid to come!* All these thoughts pulled me in, hating it. Stall after stall, then walking to another building in 98 degrees Fahrenheit and 92% humidity—sweaty, hot, carrying supplies—cleaning toilet after toilet after toilet, building after building after building.

Each day, I would try to get through it as quickly as possible, then wash up and get over to the building where the temple was. Take off my shoes, go in as quickly as possible where I could connect to the sacred—because the temple is where you connect to the sacred. This toilet thing they had me doing was totally sidetracking my spiritual awakening journey, day after day after day.

That whole first summer at the ashram, I didn't have a single breakthrough. Every day that I did toilets, day after day, I just kept trying to get through it as fast as possible so I could get to the temple where I could connect to the sacred.

Fast forward—I'm on the airplane flying to the ashram for the second summer. The whole plane ride I'm calling to Grace, saying, *Dear Divine Grace, can I please have a different* Seva? *I've done my time cleaning toilets. Let somebody else have that 'most powerful* Seva *that there is,' because it clearly didn't do me any good. Please, can I have a different* Seva?

Well, I arrived at the ashram. I went to get my *Seva* assignment. Once again: "toilet cleaning." *No! No, not again.*

That whole second summer, still not a single breakthrough. Hating it, trying to get through it as quickly as possible, then always going right to the temple afterwards to connect to the sacred.

Fast forward again—I'm on the plane ride flying to the ashram for the third summer. *Dear Divine Grace, please can I have a different* Seva? *I've done two summers of toilet* Seva. *Please, please, please.*

I arrive, go to get my *Seva* assignment. Once again, toilet *Seva. Unbelievable!*

I start asking around—veterans, people on staff—"Is it normal for someone to keep getting the same *Seva*?"

All the veterans said, "Oh no, they always mix up the *Seva* assignments so you get all kinds of experience and variety. Why are you asking?"

I said, "Well, I keep getting the same *Seva*."

They'd ask, "What *Seva* do you keep getting?"

"Toilets."

They'd giggle or try not to laugh. "Oh, so you keep getting toilet *Seva*? How's that going for you?"

"Terrible," I'd say. "I'm totally hating it, resisting it, wanting to be somewhere else. Is there somebody I could talk to, to get a different *Seva*?"

They'd say, "No. Your *Seva* is your *Seva*. Maybe there's something for you to consider here, that it keeps happening. This is not normal to keep getting the same *Seva*."

After all my research, it's now *Seva* time. We chant the opening mantra. I go into the first bathroom. As I'm walking into the first stall, I hear my inner cynic, and it actually came out of my mouth. I could hear that voice upset that once again, it's a whole other summer of this. The words that came out of my mouth as I approached the first stall to open the door: "This place has got me cleaning the throne."

When the word *throne* came out of my mouth with such intensity, it was as if some thin membrane of consciousness simply popped—like a soap bubble. In that instant, I saw that all of my suffering had been created in my own mind. I had believed there was the sacred place called the temple, where I went to connect to the divine, and then there were the "not sacred" toilets. But it was just a belief. As simple as that.

In that moment, I realized I was cleaning the throne. I am cleaning the throne for *Shiva*. Everyone is a unique expression of divine Source Essence—*Shiva*—and I am cleaning the throne for *Shiva*. This is the temple. It was bliss. It was amazing. I was suddenly so honored to be given the chance to clean *Shiva's* throne. Completely selflessly.

Previously, I had done it very selfishly, just trying to get through it as quickly as possible. Now I was in no rush. It was a different pace. I was so honored to clean each throne, one by one, so thoroughly, cleaning it for *Shiva*, divine expressions of Source Essence.

I cleaned one after another after another. It was amazing how grateful I felt to get to clean the throne, that there was no longer temple and not temple. It was all the temple, bathroom after bathroom, building after building.

The next thing I knew, the final toilet was complete. I sat back, so grateful, and realized what he had said that first summer—the person who oriented us, saying we'd been so lucky to get the most powerful *Seva* there is. He was right. It's one of the ones you would most resist. That's what he was referring to. Anything you would really resist, that you wouldn't want to do, can be a very powerful *Seva* to have a huge breakthrough. I realized I had created a construct of sacred and not sacred that wasn't actually real. It was all made up in my mind.

As I was putting the supplies away in the cabinet, everywhere I walked—every hallway, every building, every person, every wall, every floor, every ceiling—everything was an expression of *Shiva*, Source Energy Essence permeating all reality.

Next thing I know, I'm actually in the building where *the* temple is. But I'm already in the temple. Everywhere I go. I started cracking up. There it is, that place I would always rush to, feeling I had to be *in there* to connect to the sacred. I realized that everywhere we can connect to the sacred. Because it's *all* the sacred. The sacred is here, everywhere we go, within everyone and everything.

I was in the shoe room. I took off my shoes and realized: my shoes are sacred. The rack you put your shoes in: sacred. The shoe room is sacred. The hallway leading from the shoe room to the temple: sacred. I was walking at a completely different pace. No rush. Because I was already in the temple.

Then I noticed a plaque on the outside of the temple. It had always been there, but I'd never stopped to read it. I'd always been in such a rush to get inside to connect to the sacred. Now, in this new perspective, this true perspective that *everywhere is the temple*, I actually stopped and read what it said.

A temple is a sacred place in which you can so fully, directly experience your True Nature that you will come to the natural realization that all the world is the temple.

It had been there all along. I'd just never stopped to see it. That was the day I could actually understand it. Even if I'd read it before, it wouldn't have made sense. My mind would have just conceptualized it. We can only truly *know* from direct experience.

That day, in that first toilet stall, when the word *throne* came out of me, it popped the soap bubble of illusion—that there was temple and not temple. I directly experienced that *all the world is the temple.* Every day after that, I felt so honored to clean the thrones, *Shiva's* thrones.

Fast forward—I'm on the airplane flying to the ashram for the fourth summer. I'm not calling to Grace, asking for a new *Seva* assignment. It's not even in my awareness. I arrive, go to get my *Seva* assignment—fully expecting it will be toilet *Seva* because that's my *Seva.* She hands me a card. I glance at it, then look more closely. It doesn't say housekeeping.

It says: Temple.

Unbeknownst to me in that moment, I'd gotten pulled into a different kind of mind construct. The construct of: *I've graduated from toilet Seva. I must have done so well with my toilet* Seva *that now I've graduated, because I'd never get pulled into that construct again.*

But wait until you see what happened next. I walked over to the building where the temple is, holding my card that says Temple *Seva.* I was so excited: *Wow, I'm going to be doing Temple Seva. This is amazing!* I go into the shoe room, take off my shoes, about to be available for Temple *Seva,* when I hear this deep voice way down in my heart chakra: *You don't really think you're going to get to do Temple* Seva, *do you?*

I look carefully at my card to make sure I didn't misread it. It says *Temple.* I walk in, see a whole group of people, and there's someone you can tell is the Temple *Seva* coordinator. Everyone's standing there facing her. I joined the group—twelve of us, shoulder to shoulder, facing her.

She said, "Welcome everybody. Thank you so much for being willing to do Temple *Seva*. First, let me count everyone." She starts at her left, pointing at each of us. "One, two, three, four, five, six, seven . . ." (points at me) "eight, nine, ten, eleven, twelve. Those of you who are one through six, you'll be inside the temple. Those of you who are seven through twelve, you'll be outside."

Oh no. Not again! Here I am in the temple, and I don't get to do Temple *Seva*. I got pulled right back into the construct that there's temple and not temple.

We did our opening mantra. I don't even remember doing it because I was so pulled back into this whole thing. Then we went outside. Turns out outside the temple, there's a tile walkway all around the perimeter, with windows where you can see inside. They're all in there with their soft cloths, dusting the *murtis* in the nice air-conditioning.

We're outside—98 degrees Fahrenheit, 95% humidity. Our *Seva: clean the bird poop off the tile walkway.*

"This is your *Seva*—clean the bird poop." The coordinator points up. Birds fly into the rafters and poop on the walkway.

We put on full-body rubber aprons, boots, gloves, goggles, grab buckets, squeegees, scrub brushes, hoses. Sometimes someone sprays and the water splashes back on your legs — bird poop everywhere, hot, humid, sweaty—the whole time looking into the windows at them in the air-conditioned temple.

No. No. Unbelievable. I was pulled right back into the construct of sacred and not sacred. But this time, it only took three days. Not three years.

On the third day, as we went outside to clean the bird poop, I was looking at this beautiful tile walkway—how exquisite it was—and realized: *This is where* Shiva *walks. I get to clean the walkway where* Shiva *walks. This is also the temple.* The breakthrough happened again. I was released from the suffering of

my mind. I realized again: *there's only the temple.* It was amazing
—the honor of getting to clean the walkway where *Shiva* walks.

The next day we come in for *Seva*. I was so excited to clean
Shiva's tile walkway. But just before we go outside, the coordinator says, "Those of you who've been outside, you'll come
inside today. Those who've been inside will now go outside."

Right then, inside me, was such a feeling of: *Please, Divine
Grace, please shower them with blessings — those who are now
going outside. If they in any way get caught in the same suffering I
was caught in, please shower them with blessings so they too can
have this amazing breakthrough from this beautiful practice called
Seva—selfless service. Please, please, please.*

From that day on, I never got the same *Seva* assignment
again. Always something new. There were many moments later,
out on a walk, when I'd see the tile walkway had bird poop.
Even though it wasn't my *Seva*, I'd go to the cabinet and clean it.
Many times I'd see a toilet that needed attention—a throne—
and I'd clean it, even though it wasn't my *Seva*.

As the years went on, there were other *Sevas* that always
needed more help than just the three hours a day—laundry
Seva, washing dishes, especially the big pots and pans. I'd feel
the knowing to go help, even outside *Seva* time.

I felt so grateful to the practice of *Seva*, so honored to offer
up my services to this beautiful place called the ashram, where
I had received so much.

It felt so good, so wonderful, to be part of this community.
Here, we were invited to consider that every activity we are ever
involved in, in our lived human lives, can be *Seva*: an offering
from our heart. We can be selfless rather than selfish.

HONORING THE UNIQUE FEMALE
AND MALE WANTER DYNAMICS

LET'S EXPAND OUR EXPLORATION OF WATER DYNAMICS TO include the unique Wanter characteristics in males and females. There is a very unique way that the Wanter Dynamics play out in men, and a very unique way that the Wanter Dynamics play out in women. There are different characteristics for males and females.

In my role, I get to hear what it's like for women to try to navigate men, and what it's like for men to try to navigate women. I get to hear both sides, and from this perspective I can relate it back to The Wanter.

One day, I had a realization that it's very universal, and it goes way, way, back. I was imagining all the way back to the beginning of the human species.

Let's use an example. Let's say it was a northern hemisphere group of people, a tribe. It's wintertime. It's cold. They're living in a cave. There's no running water, no indoor plumbing, no grocery store, no clothing store. There are no stores at all. All day long, the tribe would have to divide up the various tasks just to survive. Conditions presented survival needs every day: water, firewood for warmth, shelter inside the cave, food sources. There was a chance of wild animals that might attack, and other various unforeseen challenges.

If we take a look at what would've naturally happened: the females—because they're the ones who have the babies—would have developed a very unique orientation. They learned how to transcend their Wanter every moment. When their baby was crying and they were tired and didn't want to tend to it, they still had to transcend their Wanter and care for the baby anyway. Otherwise, there would have been no survival of humans. The little babies would've all died. So the females had to start transcending their Wanter, letting their own needs go in favor of the baby's—again and again.

The men were out on the hunt. All of them went to track down some animal so there could be meat for the winter. The men were focused on the hunt while the babies needed tending. The women were transcending their Wanter by prioritizing the babies' needs over their own.

Meanwhile, the women were making sure there was fresh water for the tribe, gathering firewood, berries, nuts, and roots by the river, and tending to the elderly or sick. The average life span was much younger—probably about 35, based on skeletal remains of early humans. The tribe needed more humans to survive. The ability to have a baby was highly prized, deeply valued within the tribe. It was seen as a great gift. The women were honored for that, and they naturally transcended their Wanter by caring not only for their own babies, but often for others' as well.

If one woman was sick and struggling, the others pitched in to help with her babies. Survival depended on it. The women multitasked constantly—caring for the young, the sick, and the elderly, while also worrying about the men on the hunt. *Are they okay? They haven't sent smoke signals to let us know. We sure would like some sign they're safe out there.*

They were caring about the men. They were caring about

the elderly. They were making sure there was enough water, enough wood, enough berries and nuts to sustain them until, hopefully, the men came back with a downed beast so they could have meat for the winter.

This was a very different orientation for the women than it was for the men.

The men had to stay narrowly focused on the hunt. Over the years they had learned that if they got distracted—if their mind wandered to other things—they might lose track of the beast, and the beast might circle around and eat them. They developed the ability to stay focused and not let themselves drift.

There was no side talking during the hunt—it could give away their position. No conversations. Only silence. If signaling was needed, it happened through hand gestures so as not to reveal where they were. The men stayed narrowly focused on the beast, determined to bring it down and provide meat for the tribe.

This was also highly prized and valued. The men bringing back a beast meant food and survival through the winter, when other sources were scarce under snow and ice. Their ability to remain intensely focused was critical.

Now, imagine walking up to one of the men out on the hunt, tapping him on the shoulder, and asking: "How do you suppose the women and children and elderly are doing back in the cave?"

"What women? What children? What elderly? What are you talking about? There are no women, no children. There's only the hunt. Get out of here—you're distracting me. Now I've lost track of where the—No. We don't let ourselves get distracted. Get out of here."

It doesn't mean the men don't love and honor the women and the children. But in that moment, they're not even in their awareness. They can't let that be in their awareness. They have to stay very narrowly focused. That's how the male mind developed—designed to stay sharply focused.

The female mind, however, has a high multitasking orientation. Women care about the babies, other women's babies, the elderly, the water, the firewood, the berries, the nuts—all of the many things going on.

If we bring this forward to modern times, I hear the frustrations on both sides. I hear all the things men tell me about what annoys them with their female partner. And I hear all the things women tell me about what annoys them with their male partner. Part of this comes down to biology—patterns that have come down through the ages. Two different orientations.

The male mind, in general—these are broad strokes—tends to be singularly focused. When a man is on the hunt, whatever that is—whether he's at work, working from home, playing golf, on a fishing trip, or on a camping adventure—he's focused on that one thing.

All the time I hear men say things like: "Mitch, how could she not understand that I'm playing golf? How could she not understand I'm at work? Why does she need me to text her back? And if I don't text her back within 10 minutes, she gets upset. Then I start getting texts like, *Do you not care about me anymore? Do you not love me?*"

The men say, "It's not that I don't love her. I'm just focused on my work," or "I'm focused on this golf hole—I'm trying to get par here, and she's texting me while I'm playing," or "I'm on my fishing trip. That's just where my mind is." The male mind tends to be more singularly focused.

For the female mind, it's confusing: "Why is he so narrowly focused? How can he not see that the trash hasn't been taken out? We agreed he would do that. Mitch, I have to constantly remind him about the trash. How can he not see it? Why do I always have to ask him about putting his dishes in the dishwasher? Why does he never help out? Why do I have to take care of the whole cave—the whole house?"

From the men I hear: "Mitch, all she does is nag me. She doesn't notice anything I do. She doesn't give me credit for the things I take care of. It's never enough. And then, when I want intimacy, she's not interested. What's going on, Mitch? Why doesn't she want to be intimate with me?"

They don't understand what it's like for the women.

For women, it's completely different. They want the man to notice and care about the things around the house without being asked. "Mitch, how can he not see this floor is a mess? I'm busy doing fifty other things. Couldn't he just sweep the floor, vacuum, or do the dishes without me pointing it out? I do everything around here. It's like he's impervious—he doesn't even notice. And then he gets upset at me for not doing something he wanted, and now he wants intimacy? Does he not understand? That's not appealing to me at all."

In my unique role, I invite men to try to see from the female perspective, and I invite women to try to see from the male perspective.

For thousands of years, women have been the gender that had the babies. They had to learn to transcend The Wanter and care for others. Because of that, women are more naturally nurturing, more naturally looking out for others. And they can't understand why men don't get it. They ask, "Why are men so selfish? Why are they so narrowly focused?"

It's not fair to the women, but they are the ones who can help the men see where they're being selfish: not caring about the house, the children, or the details of family life. That tendency—the narrow focus of the male mind—has been there for thousands of years. Women, because they bore the babies, had to transcend The Wanter in ways men didn't.

Even if you're a woman who has never had a baby, you're still in a female body that naturally carries the DNA passed down through the ages. That wiring makes women more naturally oriented toward multitasking, more able to hold many things in awareness at once. And it often results in frustration: "How can he not see what I see?"

So it isn't fair to the women, but it is the women who help the men see what they're not seeing—to learn how to be less selfish. My role with women is to help them understand why men have this tendency, and that from the male point of view, they're under a lot of pressure.

They say, "The hunt is not easy. It's scary. I'm the one expected to protect and provide, to make sure everybody is safe, and to do everything around the house. I don't get any credit for it. Then, when I want what I want, she withholds it as a weapon. This is so unfair, Mitch. Why is she doing this to me?"

Now, if we can normalize all of this and try to have compassion and understanding for each other, we can see that there is a different Wanter Dynamic depending on whether you're in a male incarnation or a female incarnation.

To the females, I invite the possibility of understanding the male orientation that's been handed down through thousands of years of human evolution. To the men, I try to help them understand what it's like for women—how it feels to be the one doing everything around the house without ever having to be asked. Women would really appreciate it if men also noticed things on their own, without being told, and how much that small awareness endears them to you.

For men, it's helpful to understand that if you can notice what really matters to her—what makes her feel seen, heard, and properly honored—she will warm up. She'll be more open to intimacy. If, as a male, you make yourself more available to see what it's like for her, to step into her perspective, and to help out without being asked, that honoring creates connection.

To the women, I invite you to see what it feels like for the men. They feel so much pressure. They feel they have to be strong and capable, to provide and protect. Yet at the same time, they're told they need to be vulnerable, sensitive, and also notice every detail around the house: "Mitch, how am I supposed to be all of that? That doesn't make sense to me."

These are some of the characteristics I've noticed in my unique role, working with people navigating male–female relationships. If we can cultivate more compassion and understanding for each other, we can learn to accept these unique differences. We can help each other understand the ways we're wired differently. The female can help the male to understand, and the male can help the female to understand, so we can celebrate and honor those differences—and let them come together in a beneficial way.

In every moment, we can practice acceptance. That doesn't mean we're a doormat. Remember the three people in the jungle—it doesn't mean we let ourselves be walked on when our partner is doing something truly annoying. Instead, we pause and ask: *What is it my Wanter is wanting that it's not getting?*

We can use the First Growl Practice: *Oh, my Wanter is wanting him to notice that he keeps leaving cups all over the house and expects me to handle them.*

From his side, it would be wonderful for her to understand that he often feels nothing he does is enough. That no matter what he does, it doesn't get noticed. That she always seems to want more.

If we take a look at these differences and honor them, how might we open communication? How might we help each other see what we're not seeing? For men, to be more open to what it's like for their female partner. For women, to be more open to the male perspective—why he tends to operate in the world the way he does.

Then we can honor each other. We can let the love we are

be liberated in our relationship. We can have open dialogue and share a fine and wonderful adventure together. Maybe there will be less fighting and more coming together.

This is where the practices come in. When we're disturbed, if we use the Living Practice, it helps us process what's happening inside us. Then we can explore the dynamics with our partner. If we're doing the Name That Thought Practice, we're less likely to get trapped in our minds. If we're doing the Loving Blessing Practice, we're softening our hearts. Each of these practices helps us tend to our own inner work, so that when we come together, we're not simply blaming or attacking our partner from our Wanter.

This opens the door to more kindness, more understanding, more patience, more compassion. And then our relationships can flourish—becoming an adventure together, honoring the unique characteristics of males and females in this wild adventure of life on planet Earth.

THE KARMIC FIELD

WHAT IS *KARMA*? THERE ARE MANY CONCEPTS SHARED ABOUT THIS Sanskrit word, karma. I often hear people speak of it, and I'm frequently asked what it really means.

At the ashram, I was once in a class where a Swami was speaking about karma (*Swami* is a Sanskrit word meaning "teacher"). As the words the Swami shared washed over me, it felt like an energetic transmission. My attention was drawn inward, to the very center of my being. Suddenly, I had a vision: I was standing waist-deep in a smooth, calm body of water—like a pond or lake. But it wasn't just me; everyone, all beings, were standing in this same body of water. We were all connected, all sharing this water. Every small movement any of us made in the water affected all of us.

This was a beautiful metaphor for the dynamic karmic field we all share. I noticed I was holding a rock, about the size of a large lemon. I threw it into the water, and when it landed beside me, it created ripples. The ripples moved me a little, and everyone nearby was affected as well. The waves radiated outward, reaching everyone, though their effect faded the further they traveled.

Next, I held a much larger rock—about the size of a big watermelon—using both hands because of its weight. When I threw it, the waves were much bigger, and I was tossed about by the impact. Everyone near me was more strongly affected, and the ripples traveled far beyond, though again, they dissipated with distance. Then I became aware that everyone else was throwing rocks into the water too. Every action rippled through the field. It was clear that everything we do affects everything else. This karmic field, we realized, could get very turbulent if many of us were tossing many rocks.

The vision ended, and I opened my eyes, sitting among others in the meditation hall, receiving these teachings. The Swami's words rippled through the room and into the field, affecting all of us and enabling this experience. He explained that every action taken from the ego—actions that are unkind, unfair, selfish, manipulative, or controlling—creates ripples that disturb the field in a negative way. But when we connect to our true selves—that still, peaceful, loving nature—our actions do not create these harsh ripples. Instead, they soften and smooth out previous disturbances in the field.

Each moment we engage in spiritual practices—meditation, yoga, chanting, creative arts, walking in nature, witnessing a sunset, petting a puppy or a horse, hugging a baby—we connect to our natural essence, that elegant wholeness of existence. In those moments, we are not only refraining from adding negative ripples, but we are actively calming and softening the karmic ripples in the field.

This is the true invitation: to realize that in every moment, we can be this presence in the field. The more of us who connect to this True Nature, through whatever means we find, we continue to shift the dynamic karmic field we all share. Eventually, a threshold can be reached.

Ancient lineages teach that this karmic field can be influenced by our actions. When enough beings connect to love, kindness, compassion, and understanding, the field shifts in a powerful and beneficial way. At that threshold, everyone can open their hearts fully to the love and compassion that we all are. The field itself transforms, creating a new realm—a kind of earthly heaven. In such a realm, kindness, compassion, patience, and sharing would flourish. Wars would cease, starvation would end, and resources would be shared equitably. This is the lovely possibility.

The Swami shared a story of 100 people who dedicated six months to such service. They rented a building in a high-crime neighborhood in Washington, D.C., and spent their days practicing the Loving Blessing Practice, chanting mantras, and emanating loving kindness into the field. They didn't engage directly with the community or try to convince anyone to change, but their energetic presence was powerful. At the end of those six months, the crime rate in that neighborhood had dropped by 72%. Not 3%. Seventy-two percent. Just by their dedicated presence of love and compassion influencing the energetic field.

In my previous work at the Kennedy Space Center, I studied energy fields—radio waves, electromagnetic fields—and learned about field effects. Science, especially quantum physics, recognizes that everything affects everything else. This is seen in *quantum entanglement*: when two particles are linked, a change to one instantly affects the other, no matter the distance. Similarly, when those 100 people radiated loving energy into the karmic field, it affected the whole system, reducing violence and chaos.

Scientists have also studied the behavior of cryogenically frozen uranium. When cooled to extremely low temperatures (about -452°F), a liquid forms on its surface, even though only gases liquefy at that temperature. This liquid was helium. As they slowly warmed the helium back to its natural gaseous state—called *coherency*—something remarkable happened.

Just before reaching 1% coherency, the molecules in the tank were chaotic. But at exactly 1%, instant coherency occurred—the chaos vanished, and the gas became stable and unified.

This is a powerful metaphor for our karmic field.

Right now, the world feels chaotic—much like that tank just below 1% coherency. But more and more people are discovering meditation, chanting, and spiritual practices. We are approaching that crucial 1% threshold of people connected to True Nature—love, compassion, and kindness. Once we cross that threshold, the field will shift instantly. Everyone will open to their True Nature. This is described in many ancient traditions as an instantaneous awakening—a mass shift in consciousness.

This possibility invites us all to commit daily to practices that stabilize us in kindness, patience, compassion, and unconditional love. To recognize that we are not separate, but part of one elegant, dynamic whole—a vast energetic field that connects us all.

Like the vision of standing in the same body of water, every action we take ripples through the whole. When 1% of us live from love rather than separation, the karmic field will transform. There will be no more wars, no more division—only unity, compassion, and shared abundance. This is the beautiful future we are all moving toward.

Thank you for your willingness to connect each day to the kindness, compassion, and unconditional love that you are—and to remember that we are all woven together in this dynamic karmic field.

THE FRUIT TREE

WHEN I WAS AT THE ASHRAM, WE WOULD SPEAK OF *JIVAN MUKTI* AS the potential of our human expression. *Jivan* is referring to your humanness, your lived human experience, is *jivan*. *Mukti* is liberation. Liberation from the limited play of separation. Realizing oneness, directly experiencing the elegant wholeness. *Mukti* is liberation from the limiting thoughts and beliefs of the mind. Liberation from the separation construct. Realizing inherent wholeness, the oneness that everything is *Shiva*. One, divine flowing essence. You can be *mukti*, while *jivan*, while living your human life. You can be liberated. Liberated while living. *Jivan mukti*. What a lovely possibility.

My teacher at the ashram used to say, "Let's let fruit be a metaphor for *jivan mukti*. One day someone gives you a seed for a fruit tree. How fortunate is this?" She would say. "Because now you can have some fruit. How do we get this fruit? Well, we have to plant the seed that we've been given into the soil and every day, you must water it and water it. Now, if we stop watering it, we all know what happens. However, if we keep watering it every day, the seed will eventually sprout. Now, we don't see this because above the ground, there's no evidence whatsoever that anything is happening.

"Every day we water and water and water, and there's no sign of anything happening whatsoever. But underneath the ground, there's a lot that's happening. The seed is sprouting and spreading itself out nice and wide and stabilized. This takes time. This is all process. When it's nice and wide and stable and capable, when it is ready, it will now start to grow a vertical stem upward, and it will pierce the surface of the soil, come out into the open air, and little by little, that little stem will grow stronger and ever more stable, and it will become the trunk of a tree with deep roots. This tree will grow limbs and branches. And through this process, *which takes time,* it will eventually bear fruit."

She would say, "Just keep showing up for the practices. They will bear fruit."

In every moment that we are in our practices, way more is happening than we could ever imagine with our mind. There's a process, it's gradual. The practices start to build momentum the more you stay with the practices the more fruit they will bear.

In our Western culture, what we notice is we like instant results. We like to find some shortcuts, fast, hard charging ways to transform. But in the ancient lineages, we're invited to adopt a different pace. A pace of patience. A pace of patience. A patient pace. The practices will build momentum little by little. Every day, every day, we keep watering the seed.

My teacher would say over and over again, "Just keep showing up for your practices. They will bear fruit."

This is the invitation that my teacher used to give to us and that I very humbly offer to all of you that I have the great honor of exploring with. In the same way that she would invite us to just keep showing up for our practices, I invite you to do the same. *They will bear fruit.*

WISDOM OF THE PILLOW

LET'S EXPLORE THE POTENTIAL OF LETTING OURSELVES BECOME available to these practices I've been inviting you into. They give us a chance to become more stabilized—more rooted—in our True Nature, which is inherently, unconditionally loving. Our true essence is kind, patient, understanding, and compassionate. That is who we really are. These practices help liberate us, more and more, from being so easily captured by our Wanter.

Now remember, The Wanter isn't the enemy. It's always there trying to help us. It's our ally, trying to make things better for us. And yet—it's also the source of our suffering. When it's not getting what it wants, it gets disturbed. That disturbance might show up as frustration, annoyance, anger, disappointment, dissatisfaction, resentment, depression, sadness, loneliness. All of those arise when The Wanter isn't getting what it wants.

What I've seen over decades of exploring the human experience is that these practices give us a profound opportunity to become more stabilized in our true essence. When we look closely, we notice that our Wanter, especially in relationships with others, loves to be right. It clings to its rightness. And if we're stuck there, we get to be right—but we don't get to be love. Our Wanter gets to be right, but we don't get to be free. We don't get to be liberated. We just stay locked in our rightness, which keeps us separate. It becomes very hard to come together in the love that we are when we're so busy holding on to being right.

That's where these practices come in. They give us a chance to become less interested in being right, and more interested in being love.

Which brings me to a little piece of unexpected wisdom I call: Wisdom of the Pillow. Many years ago, someone I was exploring this with was in a boutique shop and saw a hand-made pillow with an embroidered phrase on it. It had no author—just these words sewn into the fabric. (Because it's anonymous, I simply call it the Wisdom of the Pillow.) It's truly the invitation of a human life. It says:

Love me when I deserve it the least, because that's when I need it the most.

Only our True Nature can live the Wisdom of the Pillow. Our Wanter can't do it. The Wanter does a version of love, but it always comes with conditions. It can't love unconditionally. It can't even *like* unconditionally. That's simply its nature—and it's not wrong or bad, it just is.

So any time someone missteps or does something we don't like, The Wanter tends to pull back love. That's how it's oriented. Most of us have grown up experiencing that kind of love—a love that's conditional. We could feel that, and we started carefully reading it, twisting ourselves into a pretzel trying to keep the love, the approval, the kindness. But when love is coming from The Wanter, it's always conditional. Eventually, we see that even the *like* was conditional. And of course, our own Wanter does the same thing. It's universal. It's part of being human.

Moment by moment, in any interaction, there's an opportunity. We can become available to the Wisdom of the Pillow. If someone is being unkind, selfish, manipulative, controlling—whatever it is—we can realize: they're just in their Wanter. That doesn't mean we let them harm us. It doesn't mean we don't speak up. We can still act, we can still set boundaries. But the best chance we have of meeting them from a different place is to return within—drop down into the heart of being inside ourselves.

What I often say in those moments is: "Please, let me be love." Then I trust whatever comes from there. That's what gives me the best chance to live the Wisdom of the Pillow.

Love me when I deserve it the least, because that's when I need it the most.

The first part—*love me when I deserve it the least.* That's when someone is in their Wanter, doing Wanter things. They might be selfish, controlling, manipulative, hurtful, unkind, uncaring. The phrase is pointing to exactly that. Can we still love them then?

The second part—*because that's when I need it the most.* When someone is in their Wanter, they're the most disconnected from the love that they are. That's when they most need to be loved. The phrase is basically saying: *When I'm in my Wanter, being icky and unkind, that's when I'm most cut off from who I really am—and that's when I most need love.*

Only our True Nature can do that. Only our True Nature can live the Wisdom of the Pillow.

Now, living this doesn't mean we're doormats. Sometimes love looks firm. Like the retired airline captain who came to my studio. The first thing he did was try to crush my hand in a handshake. In that moment, I dropped into my heart center, aligned with love. *Please, let me be love.* And my hand squeezed back firmly. That's what love looked like in that moment. If my hand could have spoken, it would've said: *Come on now. I love you too much to let you hurt me like this. We can do better. We're not going to hurt each other.* Moment to moment to moment, we can let the choice be love. And each time, it will look unique.

The practices I invite you into—Name That Thought Practice, Problem Solver Mind Practice, First Growl Practice, Living Practice, and the Loving Blessing Practice—give us the chance to become ever more stabilized in our True Nature, so we can live the wisdom of the pillow into the world.

We can love others when they're in their Wanter, and we can love our own Wanter too. We can let ourselves off the hook when we get pulled into it. Because when someone is in their Wanter, they simply can't help but do Wanter things. It's like our doggy friends. We don't expect them to be anything other than dogs. So we can still love them even when they chew up our favorite shoe or make a mess on the floor. We let them off the hook. In the same way, we can learn to let people off the hook when they're in their Wanter.

It doesn't mean we allow harm or disrespect. The wisdom of the pillow is about how we navigate those tricky moments with love. What I've found is that in those moments, I bring my attention into the heart center, align with love, and say: "Please, let me be love." And then whatever arises from there, I trust it.

From our True Nature, we can let the love we are be liberated into the world. From there, we can live the Wisdom of the Pillow.

ATMA NIDHI

ATMA NIDHI—YOU ARE A TREASURE.

Atma. In every moment of your human expression—what is actually lighting up this body, these senses, this mind, this Wanter? The bones, the ligaments, the muscles, the organs, the blood, the water. It's mostly water that we're enlivening here. Water is liquid *Shakti.* It is all *Shakti.*

Atma is our eternal essence—the unique, eternal One that we are. Each of us is a unique, divine, absolute existing presence. And we are all way beyond any of these words. There aren't really words that can describe our self-existing, pure-flowing absoluteness. It's that simple.

There is your *Atma,* lighting up the body, letting it be in on the cosmic joke.

Nidhi. Treasure. Pure treasure. The bounty of our unique divine essence. We are bountiful. We are a treasure—inherently. *Atma Nidhi.*

Every single person you interact with today—after reading this chapter, whenever you decide you're complete (you may have already stopped; maybe I'm only writing to a few who have hung in there)—everyone you've ever interacted with, everyone you will ever interact with, is also *Atma Nidhi*. A pure treasure of eternal divine essence.

If we let ourselves rest in this truth, how we are with each other shifts instantly. No more wars would come from here. No more betrayals. No more deception or manipulation. No more need for control. There would just be hugs—divine hugs—and play. So much play, when we realize everyone is *Atma Nidhi*.

A pure treasure of divine, eternal existence, experiencing a human form that, yes, will still have a Wanter. Until that cosmic shift where everyone fully opens, we're still going to have this Wanter that does Wanter things. And we can accept that. When we're with each other, we can honor that who we really are is *Atma Nidhi*—this pure treasure of our eternal essence—we can also honor that everyone's having their own human experience.

Now, many, many more people are opening, resting back, and becoming interested in ways—natural ways—to directly experience *Atma Nidhi*, the treasure that they are. The more we abide in that, through our practices, the more it reveals itself.

The practices I offer—from my own direct experience—are simple ways to become less captured by thought. The Name That Thought Practice is so beautiful for this. It gives us a chance to shift the habit of our attention so we're not so lost in the mind. We're not saying the mind is wrong or bad. We honor the mind. Its job is to solve problems. So we let it. But so much of the time, there isn't actually anything that needs solving. With Name That Thought Practice, we honor the mind. We name the thought, but we don't chase after it.

Remember, it emerged from the cat-mouse meditation I learned at the ashram: we were invited to be the cat—sit attentively, see if a mouse comes out of the hole. If a mouse does, we don't chase it. We simply notice what kind of mouse it is, then rest back and see if another comes. Same with the mind. The very first time I ever shared this, instead of teaching her the cat-mouse meditation, I said: *Be on the lookout for your next thought.*

If one comes, tell me what it's inviting. It invited her into a state of wonder about the mind. Let's be in wonder. Are there thoughts that come? Are there little mice? If so, let's honor them. Let's name them. We don't have to chase them. Because if we chase them, we get pulled into the story. When we do Name That Thought, we name the thought and rest back, and see if another comes. And if another comes, we honor it, name it, rest back again.

What are we resting back into? *Atma Nidhi.* The treasure. The pure treasure of our divine essence. Our eternal *Atma Nidhi.* Yes. The treasure of our pure essence.

The Living Practice is for when we do get pulled in. Because that's going to happen. Thoughts will come, they'll pull us into a story, that story stirs emotions, and now we're on the ride. We're affected. We're feeling intense feelings. That's part of our human experience. So we honor that. We don't try to figure it out, solve it, change it, or stuff it down. We just let ourselves directly experience that energy—that *Shakti.* Because that's what emotions are: *Shakti* of a certain frequency, showing where The Wanter is wanting something it's not getting. That's what creates frustration, annoyance, anger, resentment, disappointment, sadness. All of these emotions are just *Shakti* that contracted because our Wanter resisted life—wanted it to be some other way, wanted it optimized for us. That's where those feelings come from. So when that happens, that's okay. That's part of the play. We honor it. We let ourselves feel it in the body. Not to analyze it, distract from it, or stuff it, but to just let it be experienced directly—knowing it's all *Shakti.* We let it flow like an energy river, and also remember: that's not all we are. That temporary flow of *Shakti* we call emotion is not all we are. Because we are also *Atma Nidhi.* This treasure of pure awareness. This divine, unique essence.

Then there's the Loving Blessing Practice. The third of the three essentials. Yes, there are other practices I offer, but these three—Name That Thought, Living Practice, and Loving Blessing—are fundamental. Practices like First Growl, Problem Solver, or Viveka are more on-the-fly practices—ways to meet moments as they arise. But these three primary practices—Name That Thought, Living Practice, and Loving Blessing Practice—are like the three sturdy legs of a stool. They're the pillars that hold everything up. They stabilize us, give us a reliable foundation so that when The Wanter inevitably does Wanter things, we have a way to meet it.

With Loving Blessing, we instantly get in touch with a being we can easily love. Maybe it's an animal or a person. And we let the love that we are be shared. Naturally emanated, given—no attachment to outcome. It just loves. Doesn't need to be loved back. This is our True Nature. We are this treasure that loves, that is pure, that is eternal awareness, and also pure love. Sometimes we're resting more in the pure awareness aspect of what we are. In Loving Blessing, we get to directly experience the absolute love that we are—love with no conditions.

This practice is so revealing. Because if someone comes into our awareness that our Wanter has a disturbance with, we get to see: do we withhold love from them? If we do, that's okay. Don't judge or blame yourself. That's just The Wanter. The Wanter holds grudges, keeps grievance lists. Whenever someone didn't do what we wanted, The Wanter adds it to the list, and then feels justified in withholding love.

In the Loving Blessing Practice, if we can't send the love, that's okay. We just gently return to someone we *can* beam love to. Little by little, it builds momentum. And we'll notice we become less and less interested in being right, in holding onto our grievance lists—and more interested in being love. The love gets liberated. Yes.

When we add in chanting, it tunes this bio-organic sensory vehicle we call the human body. It tunes the instrument so it can play the music it's meant to play.

These are the essentials. The main practices offered here. This book is a way to get to know The Wanter, the dynamic play it is in with our True Nature, how it gets us to thinking it's all of who we are. And these three primary practices are how we return again and again to who we really are.

Atma Nidhi. This love. This pure awareness. This presence that we are. This eternity that we are. It gets liberated. Lived. Shared.

Atma Nidhi.

ACKNOWLEDGMENTS

When we choose to enter into a human life, it's like going on an adventure into an unknown land of mystery and forgetting and buck wild situations and circumstances. I would like to thank all of the people that have helped me in my journey here. To all of you, I am so grateful for all that you have been willing to share with me along the way. It has allowed this offering that I playfully call *Wanter Dynamics & The Love We Are*. It is simply what I've noticed and have found helpful along the way, and I offer it to anyone who might also find it useful.

My gratitude starts with my mom, Marion Louise Adams. Thank you mom for the unconditional love that just so naturally poured from your heart to me and to Kelly, my sister and Marsh, my brother, and to all who knew you for all the ways that you invited me into the direct experience of the majesty of existence. Thank you for all the love. I've come to realize over the decades that this foundation of unconditional love that you so naturally provided for me is really quite rare in human life.

Thank you to Aria Devi. This book wouldn't have happened without her. She made it very clear to me that there was a book in all of these audios. She could feel it, could sense it, and she knew that she was to transcribe the audios and be available to the lovely possibility of this book. It wouldn't have happened without her, and all of her efforts, and all of her love, and all of her kindness. Thank you so much. I am so grateful to you.

Thank you to my four sons. As my guru said to me one day at the Ashram, "four Sons can change the world." Absolutely.

Thank you to Wes and Blake and Alan and Neil. I love you all with all my heart and I have learned way more from you, than you have ever learned from me. You are four amazing men, sharing your natural gifts into the world. Thank you for all that you are. Thank you for how you have touched my heart in my life. I am so grateful. Thank you to Ginger who I was married to for 35 years, I have always loved you with all my heart. Thank you Kelly for always being such a living embodiment of unconditional love. To Marsh, you are so kind and so patient and you are such a treasure!

Tory Dube Green, thank you for your loving care and dedication in editing this book and making the accompanying audio recordings accessible. Your thoughtfulness and attention have helped this offering truly shine. I am deeply grateful for your support throughout this journey.

Thank you, Jetter Green, for your beautiful artistry in designing the cover that now holds these words. Your generous heart shaped the visual invitation, and I am so grateful for your wonderful contribution.

Leslie Rapparlie, thank you for bringing your passion and expertise to the final edits. Your care and insight shaped this book in such meaningful ways, and I'm truly grateful. This book is stronger, more accessible, and more alive because of your generous contribution.

Thank you to my teacher at the ashram and all seven summers at the ashram, all of the ancient practices and wisdom teachings and ancient texts and your natural ways; the love that you are. I am so grateful to you, Guru. My journey with you is the very natural way that I share in this playfully written offering called *Wanter Dynamics & The Love We Are*.

Thank you so much to all of the Swamis at the ashram that I learned from. I am so grateful to you. Thank you to the eleven more teachers that I had the great honor of sitting with and learning from in the four years after my seven years at the ashram. To all of you, I am so grateful. I learned so much. Thank you so much. I apologize to all of you, if I share anything in this book that I don't give you credit for. Please know that that was never my intention. I always try to give credit to who I learned something from, so if I did share anything that came from you and I didn't acknowledge it, please know that in my heart and in the very essence that I am, I am so grateful to you for all that I received from all of you.

Finally, thank you to all of the people that I have had the great honor of sitting with and exploring the very nature of human life, together. All of you, all these decades in these wonderful three hour or more explorations that we do together that I continue to have the great honor of experiencing with all of you. I have so much gratitude for you, and there are so many of your wisdoms that are in this book as well. Thank you all so much.

All I know for sure is that I love you all with all my heart.

GLOSSARY

For reference, this glossary provides brief descriptions of key Sanskrit words and practice names used throughout the book.

Throughout the text, simplified forms of Sanskrit words are used to support ease of pronunciation. Each glossary entry also presents the standard transliteration and the Devanāgarī script for accuracy and reference.

All teachings in this book are transcriptions of live recordings by Mitch Rosacker, preserved as authentic spoken offerings. For those who wish to experience the original recordings, they are available on all major streaming platforms, YouTube, and at TheLoveWeAre.com.

Ānanda (आनन्द): Bliss, equanimity, wonder, playfulness, creativity, naturalness.

Ātmanidhi (आत्मनिधि): *Ātma* (each person's unique eternal spiritual essence, soul) + *Nidhi* (Treasure, the inner treasure of the True Self).

Citi / Chiti (चिति): The divine flowing essence permeating all reality.

First Growl Practice: An invitation to honor and observe The Wanter, thank it for wanting whatever is occurring to be different than it is. Allowing us to rest back in our True Nature and navigate that moment free from the made suffering that would have occurred had we gotten captured in The Wanter.

Jīvanmukti (जीवन्मुक्ति): Liberated while living in the body.

Karma (कर्म): Action or deed. The cause and effect relationship of reality. "Everything that occurs affects everything that occurs."

Living Practice: An invitation to honor and directly experience our feelings without trying to fix, analyze, solve, or distract from them. We then realize the feeling is not all that we are and directly experience the awareness of the feeling, which is not being affected at all. If practiced regularly it reduces the made suffering that we experience when we do get identified with and captured in our feelings.

Loving Blessing Practice: An invitation to directly experience the love we are and allow it to be shared as a blessing. If practiced regularly it liberates us from the grievances our Wanter gathers up in our journey of life, that we have toward others, and liberates the love we are.

Loving The Little One Practice: An invitation to honor the little fragile one within all of us. Bringing absolute unconditional love and embrace to this little one which reveals that the love our little one has been looking for outside ourselves, can only truly be found within. If practiced regularly our little fragile one comes to rest in the love we are.

Mantra (मन्त्र): Sacred sound or phrase used for meditation or invocation. An alive vibration of the truth.

Mūrti (मूर्ति): Image, statue, or form embodying the divine; an enlivened object.

Namaḥ (नम:): "I bow," "I honor," "I welcome," or "I let go"; an expression of reverence.

Namaste Mudrā (नमस्ते मुद्रा): The gesture of joining the palms at the heart as an expression of respect and devotion.

Name That Thought Practice: An invitation to honor and observe the mind. If practiced regularly it changes the habit of our attention from being so likely to get captured in our thoughts and reduces made suffering.

Oṃ (ॐ): The primordial sound of all reality. The sound of the universe. The song of existence.

Preyas (प्रेयस्): Choosing what is temporarily pleasurable and immediately gratifying (Wanter choices).

Problem Solver Mind Practice: This practice allows us to notice when Problem Solver Mind has gone forward in time or back in time to solve either something it sees may be a problem for us in the future, or sees something that has already occurred as a problem in the past. And it will relentlessly attempt to solve it, which could lead to anxiety and fear or shame and guilt. If practiced regularly it changes the habit of our attention from getting pulled into the future or past and reduce made suffering.

Pūjā (पूजा): Both the ritual of offering to the Divine and the altar space where those offerings are placed.

Sat (सत्): The eternally existing Truth, pure being, or absolute reality.

Sādhanā (साधना): Spiritual practices; being in a life of spiritual practices.

Śakti / Shakti (शक्ति): Divine power, energy, or creative force. The Divine energy permeating all reality.

Śiva / Shiva (शिव): The Divine primordial essence from which everything emerges. A principal deity representing pure consciousness.

Śivāya / Shivaya (शिवाय): "To Shiva"—used in mantras as an offering. The true essence that I am which is within everyone and everything.

Śreyas / Shreyas (श्रेयस्): Choosing that which is truly beneficial to ourselves and others. The higher, ultimate good leading to liberation (True Nature choices).

The Wanter: An aspect of human consciousness that comes into being at birth to ensure our survival. Its function is to do whatever it takes to make things better for us without regard for others. It is the root of all of our suffering *and* it is our ally. By the way . . . it is not the villain of this story.

True Nature: What we already are. What we have always been. What we will always be.

Viveka (विवेक): Refined discernment; which contains two components, Shreyas and Preyas.

ABOUT THE AUTHOR

Mitch was raised in a small Colorado farm town by a naturally mystical single mom who shaped his lifelong path of wonder. He became a pilot and earned degrees in Aeronautical Science and Avionics, completing his studies at Embry-Riddle Aeronautical University. While working as an engineer on NASA's Space Shuttle Program and projects like the Hubble Space Telescope, a spiritual awakening redirected his path from outer space to inner space. He earned a master's degree in Transpersonal Counseling Psychology and Art Therapy from Naropa University followed by decades immersed in ancient wisdom, studying with gurus and spiritual teachers of many traditions. Today, at Self Discovery Studio in Colorado, Mitch shares direct experiences, practices, and stories that invite others to directly experience their True Nature!